Hi,

Thank you for the purchase of this workbook. Doing simple drawings with pen and ink is a very relaxing and enjoyable hobby, and with this workbook, you will soon discover how easy it is as well.

"So, what can I draw in limited time I get from my busy schedule" is a question I most often get asked and this workbook is my attempt to answer it.

The focus in this workbook is on a process with clear steps that can be used to draw quick pleasing landscapes in short time. Limitless variations on this 'theme' are possible and a different pleasing landscape can be easily drawn from imagination once the steps are understood and practiced. The size of resulting landscapes can be as small as 2 by 3 inches and finished in under 10 minutes in your quick breaks. Or it can be bigger with more elements and details. The choice is yours. Important thing to understand is that behind anything that looks quite involved as a final product, there are simple steps that are used to put it together. Same is true with drawing landscapes. Here we will look at those steps for drawing landscapes in fully illustrative way with hands on exercises. Draw them for yourself, or in a thank you card for your friends or just doodle them in the margin of your journals. These drawings will let you relax, get you imagining going and will immensely satisfy you with quick pleasing results.

Do try different activities in the workbook. You can supplement it by additional practice on your own drawing book. If the initial attempt is not to your liking, then try again. Don't get discouraged in the beginning and take break between attempts if you need to. Once you start, you will discover the joy of putting pen on paper and creating simple pleasing landscapes from your imagination.

Happy Drawing,

Rahul Jain
www.pendrawings.me

Note on Pen and Paper:

So, what is a good pen for drawing?

For activities in this workbook, I would recommend a good quality fine tip gel pen. Since the size of drawings covered in this workbook is small, a fine tip (0.5 mm or less width) would be appropriate. Normal writing pens are usually medium tip (0.7 mm width or more) and this nib size isn't suitable for drawing at small size.

Gel pens are ideal for beginners as a good quality fine tip gel pen from a reputable brand can be had at a very reasonable price from most stores and gel ink is sufficiently dark and fluid to give nice drawing results. Another great option is 'fine liners', which you can easily find with fine tip. One very popular brand is 'Pigma Micron', but to reiterate, any good fine point gel pen or marker/fine liner will do in the beginning.

I would suggest not using pencil. Most pencils don't give sufficiently dark lines that you need to create texture with lines alone. Permanence of pen lines also promote good observation and avoid 'draw-erase-draw' cycle that frustrates many beginners. Use of ordinary ball pen is also discouraged as their ink is not dark enough to enable proper texturing. As you progress in your journey and you desire better quality pens for drawing, you can check out my website and videos for more information.

www.pendrawings.me/penpaperchoices

As for paper, in addition to this workbook, any normal paper like the one you use for normal printing will do. Avoid textured paper as this will interfere with flow of nib. Choose a smooth paper instead. There is again an incredible variety of paper available for drawing and you can find discussion on relative merits of these for pen and ink drawing at the above link.

Note on Proper Use of Pen for Drawing:

A key aspect of drawing with pen is to let your pen float on the paper with the nib/tip touching and releasing ink.

Never dig into the paper by pressing nib/tip in the paper.

Hold your pen lightly and release the tension in your hand. This will help you get the freedom of pen movement and lightness that contributes to good drawing practice.

A good quality gel pen and marker will provide a nice line with gentle touch on paper. If you find that you need to dig to get the ink out, then change the pen. 'Forcing' ink out of pen is never recommended. It will ruin drawing paper and create hard lines and ruin the drawing experience for you.

In the following pages, different pen strokes are illustrated that can be used to convey different textures. When attempting them, keep your hand supple and most importantly, keep it moving. The stroke shouldn't be done in a slow and deliberate manner, as this makes it rigid and un appealing. At the same time, don't rush through it. Find your speed and rhythm at which the pen line has a natural appeal. This takes time and practice and you will soon find yours.

Please note that all drawings and content in this workbook is my copy right and solely provided for your own personal use. It can't be used, resold or redistributed in any manner without my prior consent for any purpose other than personal use. As a pen and ink artist, my aim is to promote pen and ink drawing as a creative and relaxing hobby for all but please make sure that you obtain my consent before using the material in this workbook in any manner other than personal use.

For other workbooks in this series, please visit www.pendrawings.me/workbooks

Dedicated to all who seek to discover and express their creative side

Version 2, December 2020

Do make use of all the space in this workbook and practice doing all the activities. As with mostly everything else, practice is the key to improving. If you don't like your initial attempt, then don't get discouraged and try again. Enjoy the process of discovering your creative side

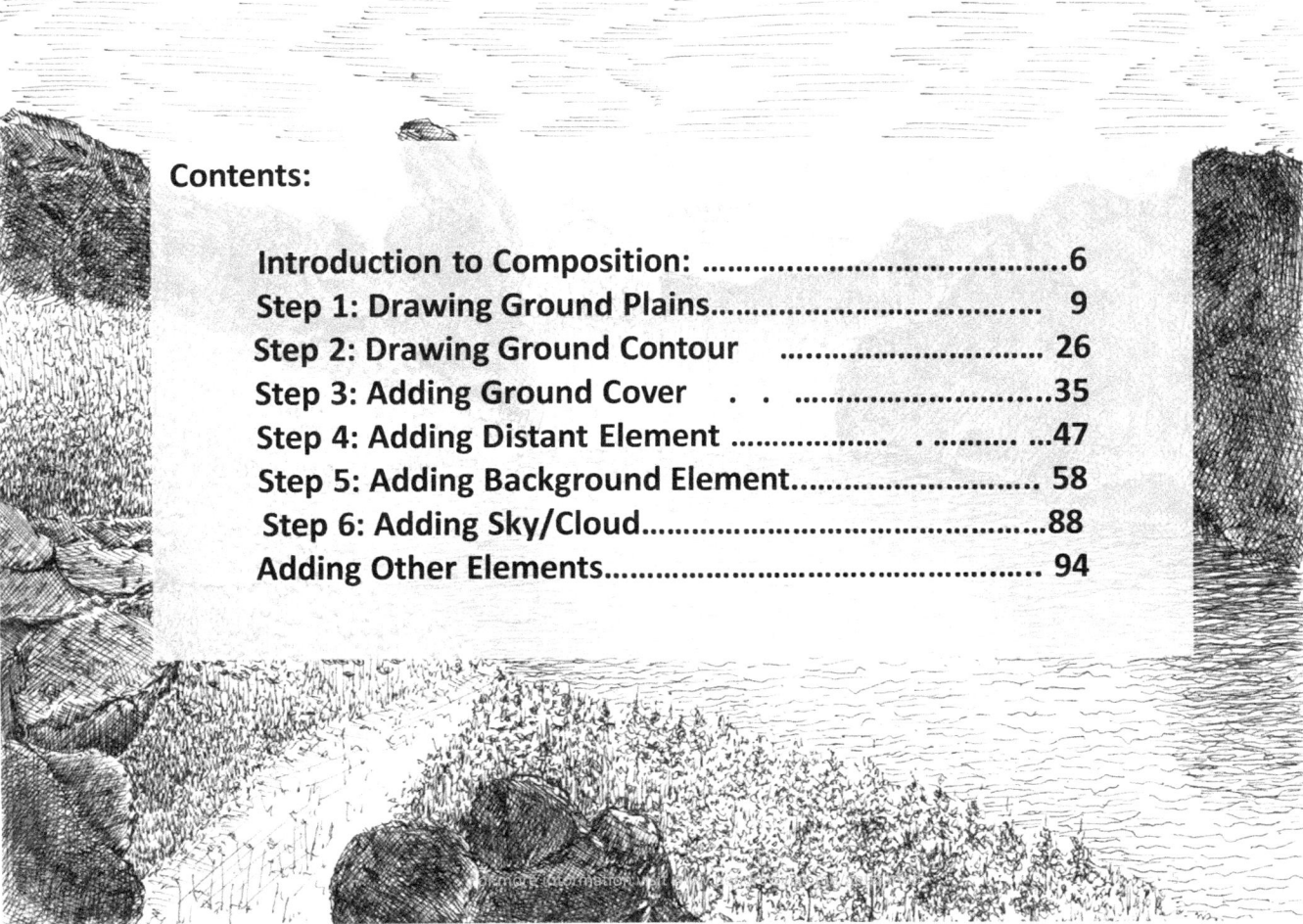

Contents:

Introduction to Composition: 6
Step 1: Drawing Ground Plains...................................... 9
Step 2: Drawing Ground Contour   26
Step 3: Adding Ground Cover 35
Step 4: Adding Distant Element 47
Step 5: Adding Background Element............................ 58
Step 6: Adding Sky/Cloud...88
Adding Other Elements... 94

Main Elements in a Simple Landscape:

Lets start by looking at the main elements of drawing a simple pleasing landscape. We will next look at these elements in detail. Notice how by combining these elements, a pleasing feel is obtained in the drawing.

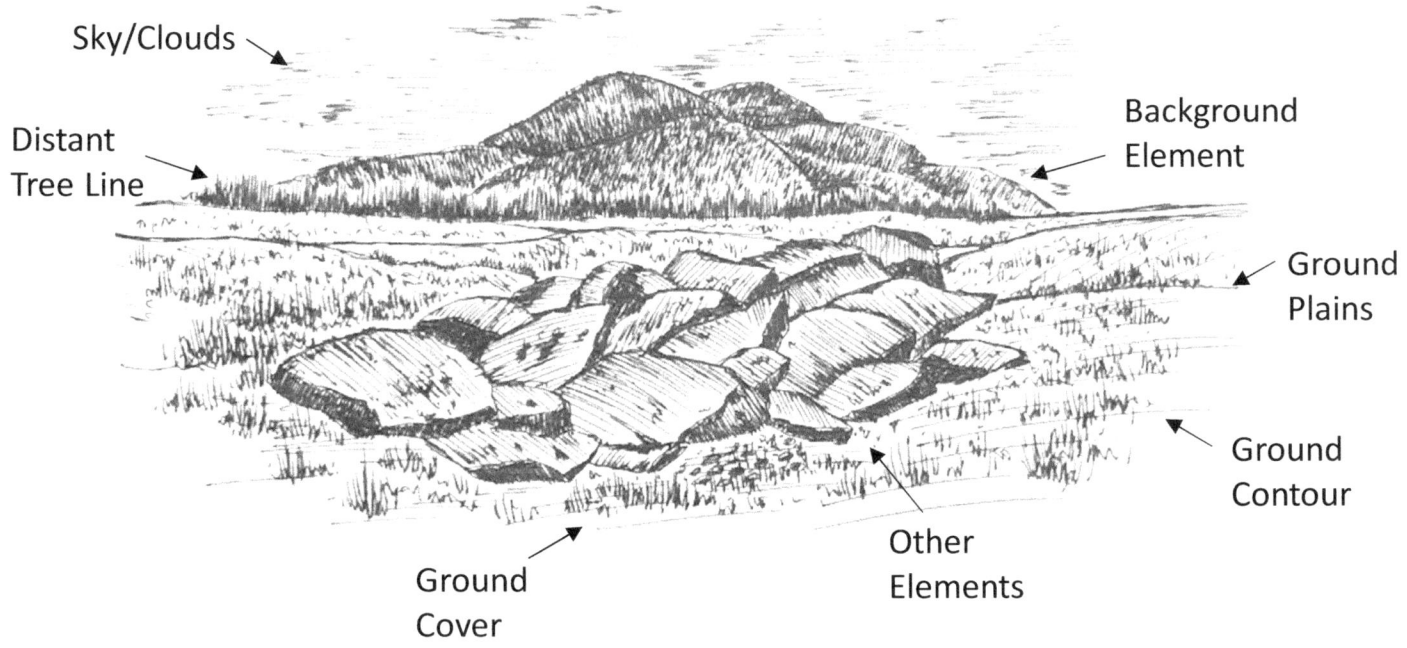

Concept of 'Organic Line':

An organic line is obtained by holding pen gently and giving pen a gentle movement. It has a soft and mellow appearance as seen below. In contrast, a 'hard line' results when pen is held tight and moved in slow deliberate manner.

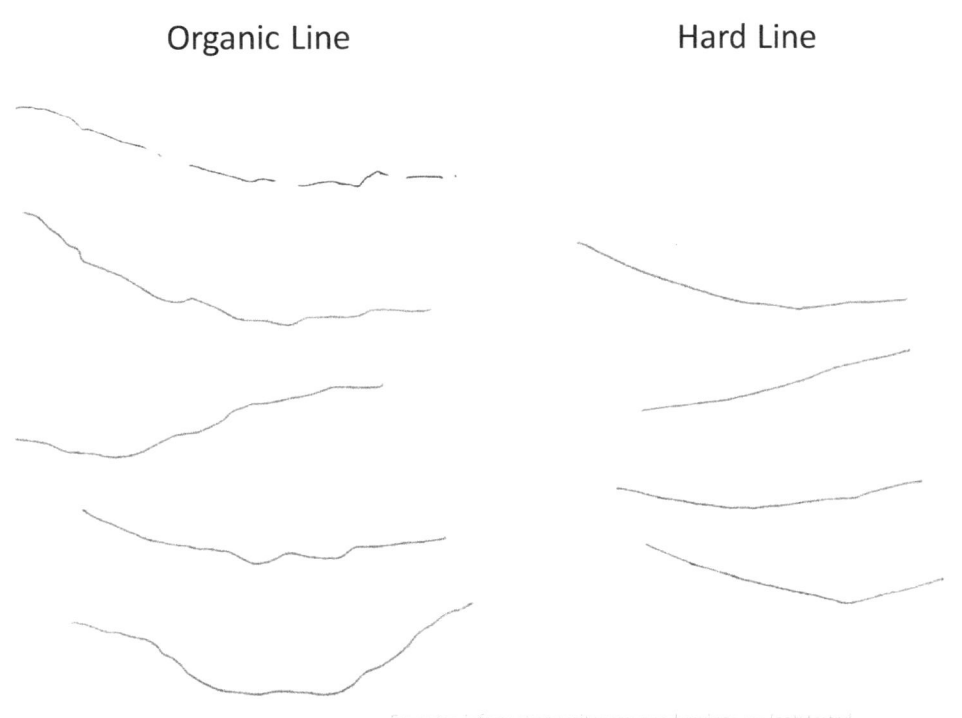

Organic Line   Hard Line

When drawing plains and other elements of a landscape, always use organic lines to draw their outlines.

Concept Of Different 'Grounds':

Depending on how far an object or ground is from the viewer, it is considered as either a background (farthest out), foreground (closest to the viewer) or a middle ground (in between foreground and background). First step in a composition is defining how the ground is shaped from foreground to background.

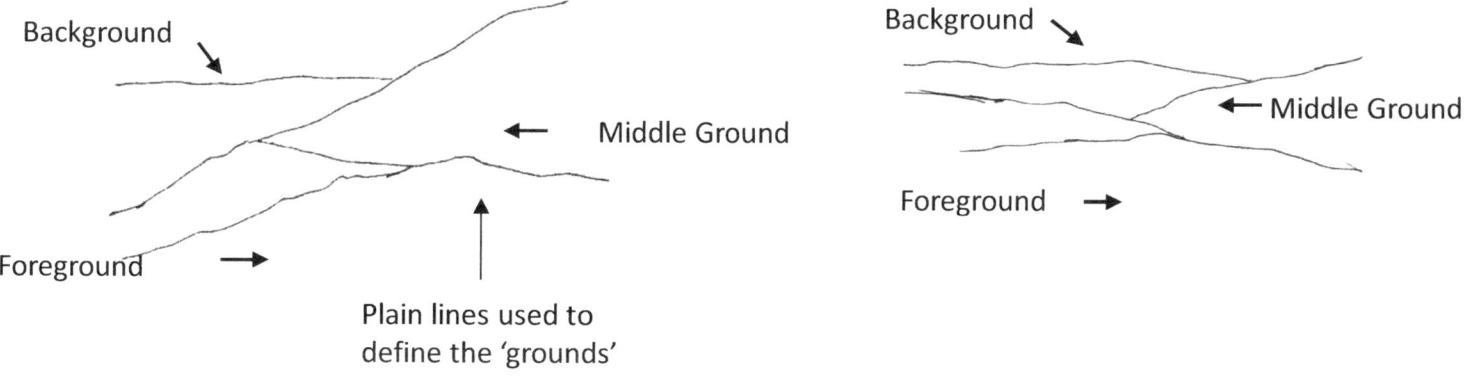

Step 1: Drawing Ground Plains:

A 'Plain' refers to a piece of land that is oriented in a certain way. The ground in our composition is comprised of different plains that run from foreground to background. A plain is specified by using **'Plain Lines'**. In the first step, we use 'plain lines' to organize the ground into different plains. The plain line that is at the top (furthest out) is usually the 'horizon' and represents far out background. Space in front of plain line closest to viewer is the foreground.

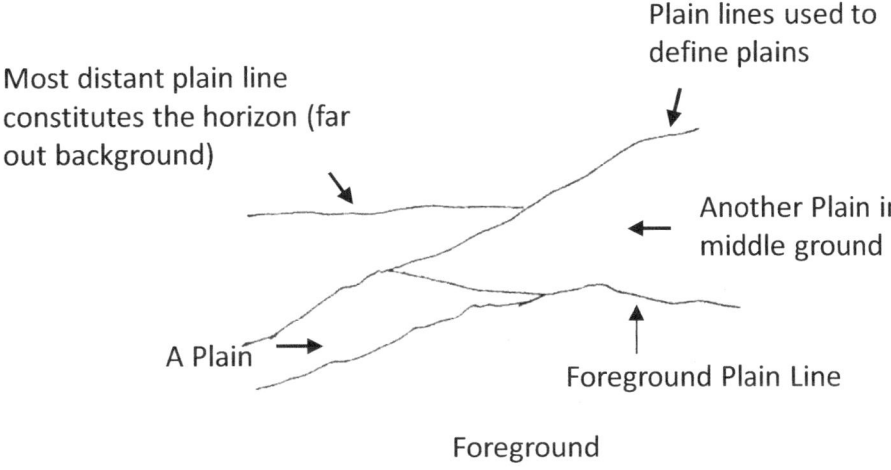

Drawing Ground Plains, Start with Horizon:

In the beginning, it is good to proceed in order from background to foreground or vice versa. Start from the background by initially drawing a background plain line or 'Horizon' .

A single like this represents horizon, or the far out distance.

Some more examples of distant horizon. This kind of curved organic line works well for a distant horizon.

Drawing Ground Plains, Adding Middle Ground:

Next add more plain lines below horizon plain line to create additional plains representing middle ground.

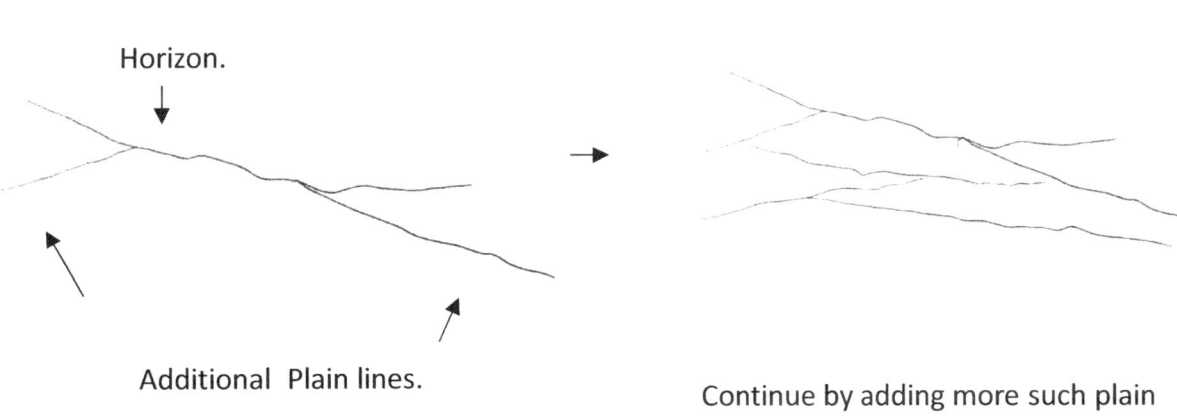

Horizon.

Additional Plain lines.

Continue by adding more such plain lines to create middle ground plains.

Drawing Ground Plains, Adding Foreground:

Finally add plain line to define the foreground. This complete the drawing of ground plains.

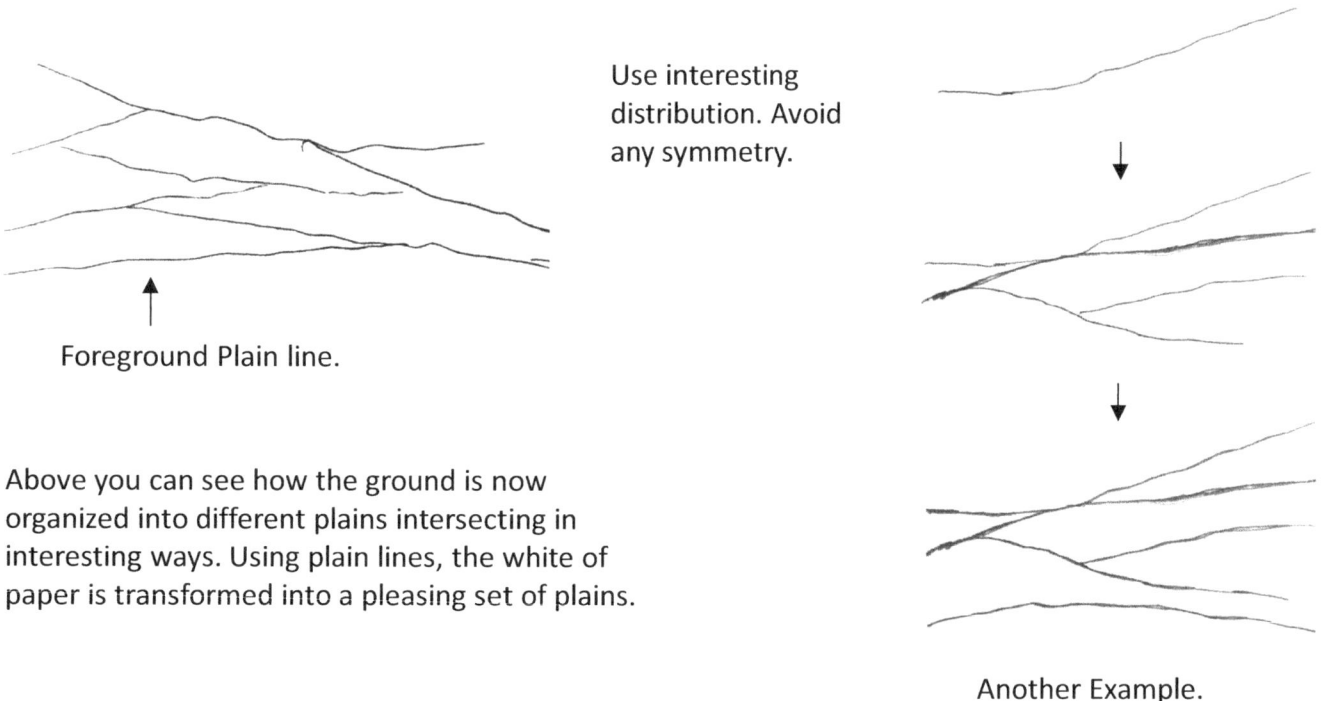

Foreground Plain line.

Use interesting distribution. Avoid any symmetry.

Above you can see how the ground is now organized into different plains intersecting in interesting ways. Using plain lines, the white of paper is transformed into a pleasing set of plains.

Another Example.

Drawing Ground Plains, From Foreground to Background:

Plain lines and hence plains can be created starting from foreground and going to background as well. In fact, with experience, you will be able to draw them interactively.

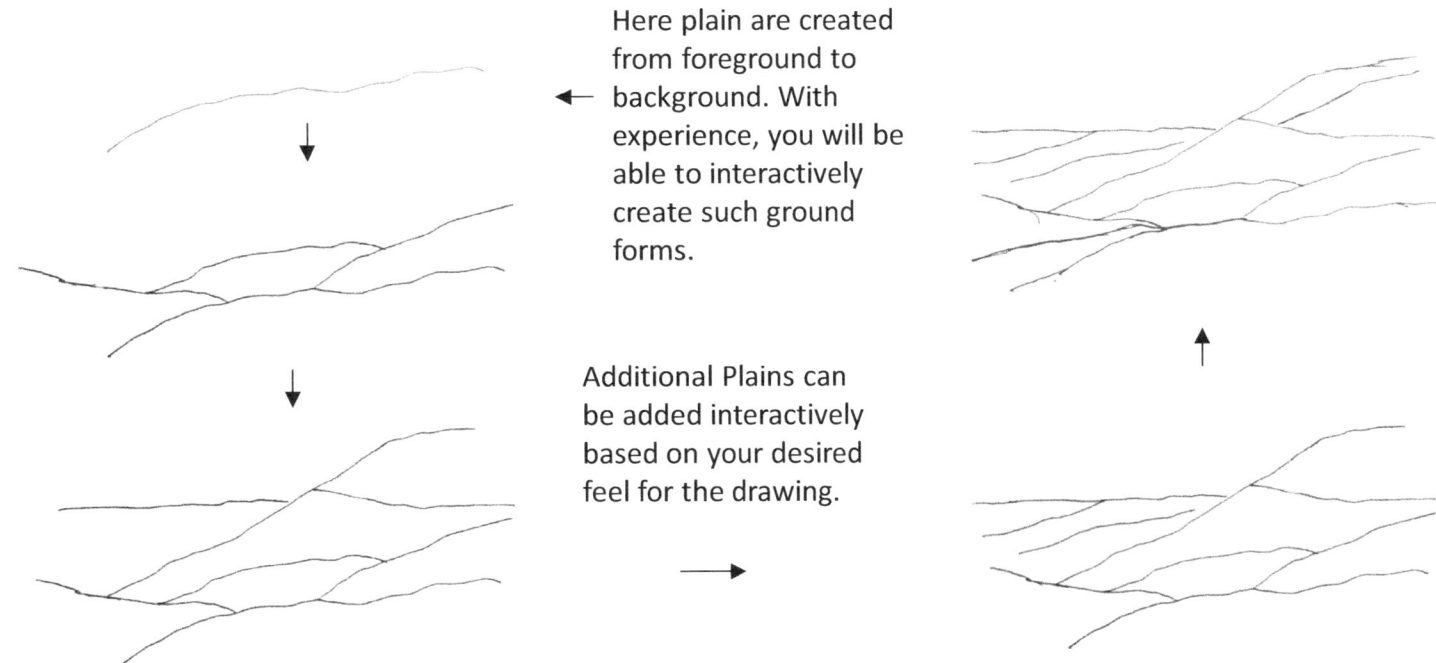

Here plain are created from foreground to background. With experience, you will be able to interactively create such ground forms.

Additional Plains can be added interactively based on your desired feel for the drawing.

More Examples:

Here are some more examples. Notice that there is a sense of balance between the sides. Keep it bit asymmetrical to add energy and interest. Avoid symmetric plains as it looks unnatural and unappealing.

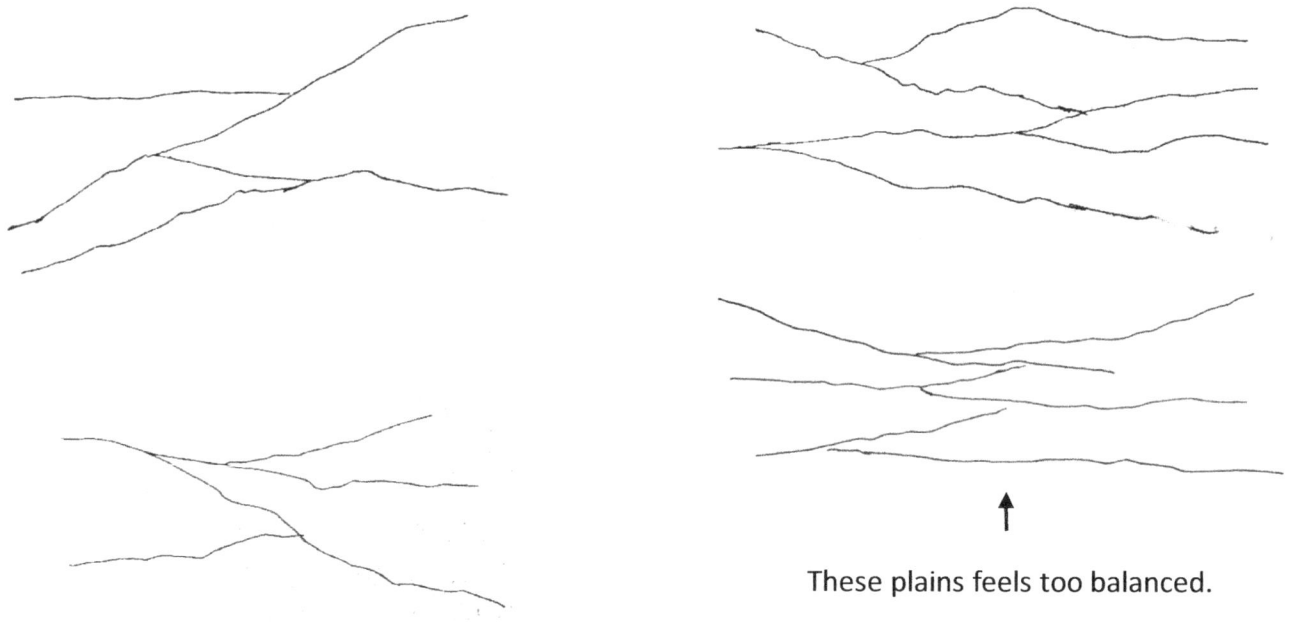

These plains feels too balanced.

Perspective Consideration:

Per perspective, things become smaller as they go out in the distance. Same holds true for plains farther out closer to horizon. Bigger plains closer to horizon makes it look flat. Plains becoming smaller with distance reinforces perspective and give sense of distance as well.

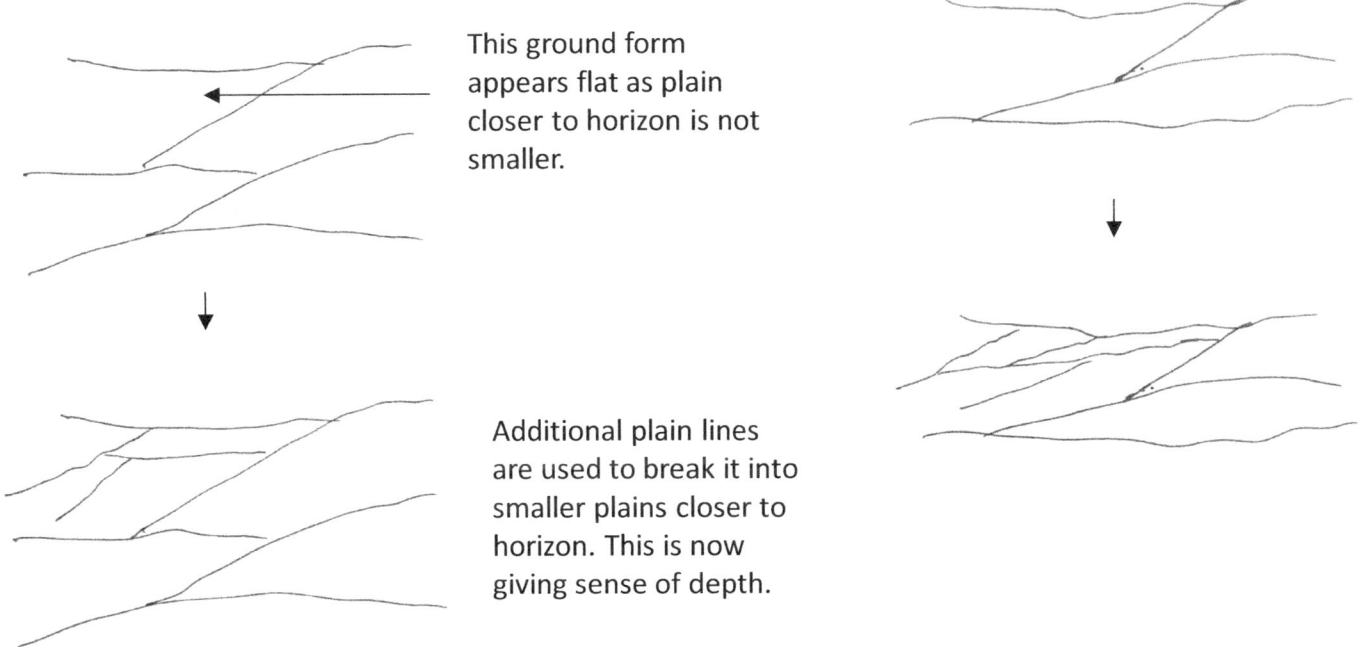

This ground form appears flat as plain closer to horizon is not smaller.

Additional plain lines are used to break it into smaller plains closer to horizon. This is now giving sense of depth.

Drawing Cross Shaped Interesting Plains:

In the beginning, following approach can be used to create interesting plains. As you get more experience, you will be able to create them from your imagination on the fly.

Start by drawing the closest foreground plain line first. Add receding diagonally intersecting plain lines to define middle ground.

Add more receding plain lines to your liking. Vary the angle to make it interesting.

Finally draw the distant horizon.

Open vs Overlapping Plains:

**If a plain line starts from edge of another plain line, then resulting plain is partially hidden behind other plain.
If the plain line is not starting from edge of another plain, then it is results in an 'open plain'.**

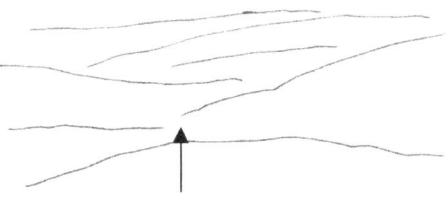 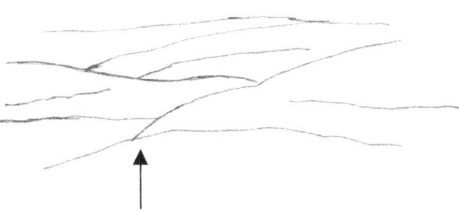

As the plain line is not touch other plain line, the resulting plain doesn't have a feel of being partially hidden behind the front plain.

Extending the plain line to edge of other plain line makes the resulting plain partially hidden behind the plain in front.

Other open plains are also added. Such mix of overlapping and open plains is usually visually appealing.

Complexity of Ground Form:

Few plain lines can be used to create ground form with few bigger plains. More plain lines can be added to create smaller and smaller plains resulting in quite complex ground form. The right level of round form complexity will be dictated by what other elements you intend to use and focus of your composition. There is no right or wrong. Experiment with different choices to see their interplay.

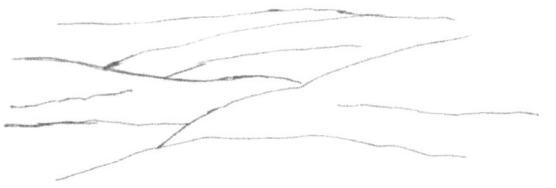

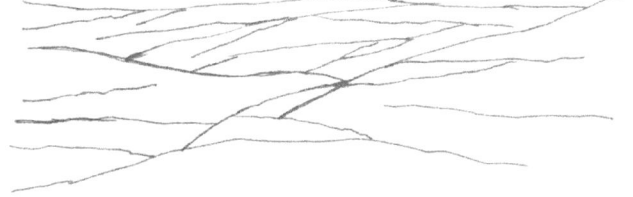

This is the ground form we saw before. This level is sufficient for most drawings.

Here the plains are further sub divided. If ground is the main focus of drawing, then such complex form can be useful.

Later we will also look at use of more curved plain lines to create more interesting ground forms.

Activity: Drawing Ground Plains:

Following are some starting points. Add more plains to them to finish their ground forms. Draw one of your own.

Perspective Rule for Elements on Ground:

Size of an object decreases as it goes out in the distance. Objects in foreground are drawn bigger than same object in middle ground. Objects in background are smallest. This also depends on the natural size of the object. A mountain in background is still drawn bigger than a stone in foreground.

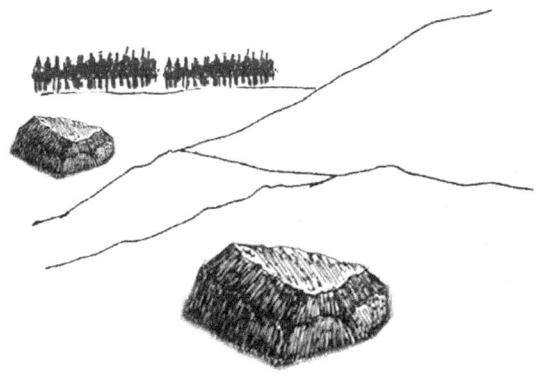

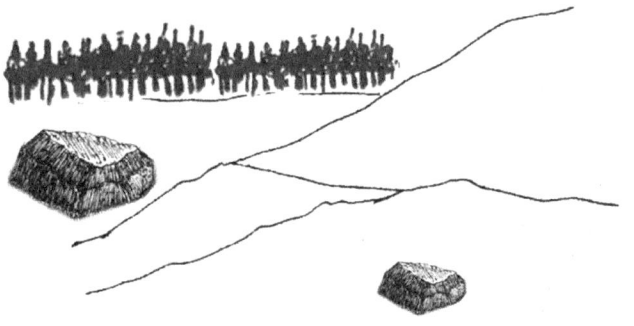

Feels Right. Foreground Stone is bigger than middle ground stone and distant trees are small.

Feels Wrong. Foreground Stone is smaller than middle ground stone and distant trees are bigger than what we expect.

Make Sure It Looks Natural:

Size of different elements in your drawing should work together and feel 'natural'. A young tree in foreground would be smaller than a mature tree in middle ground. So the perspective rule is to help you in drawing elements at right size, but in the end, the drawing should look natural.

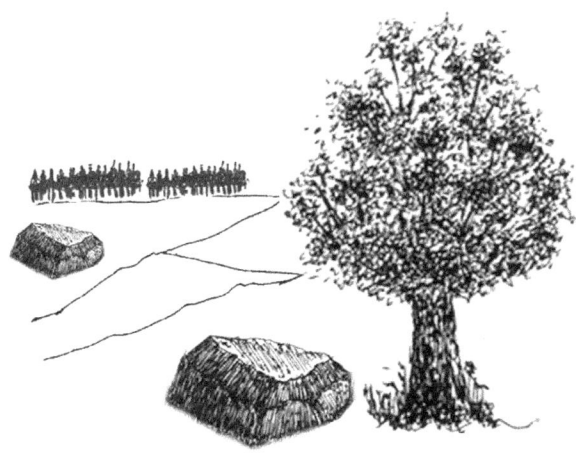

Bigger size of foreground elements (tree and stone) makes them feel very close to viewer.

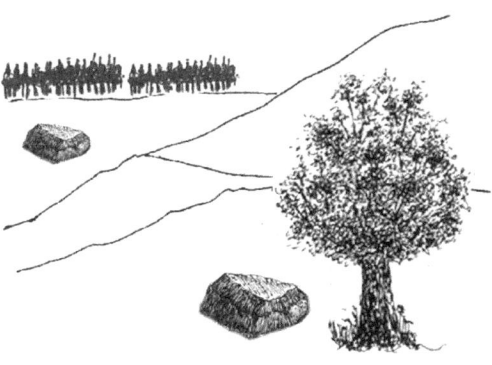

When elements closer to viewer are drawn smaller, then tend to be perceived in middle ground. Foreground here is implied with no elements.

Perspective Rules: Some More Examples

Study the examples below to understand how size of an object changes as it moves into different 'grounds'. Again, there is no hard and fast rule about the magnitude of change in size. Makes sure the drawing looks natural.

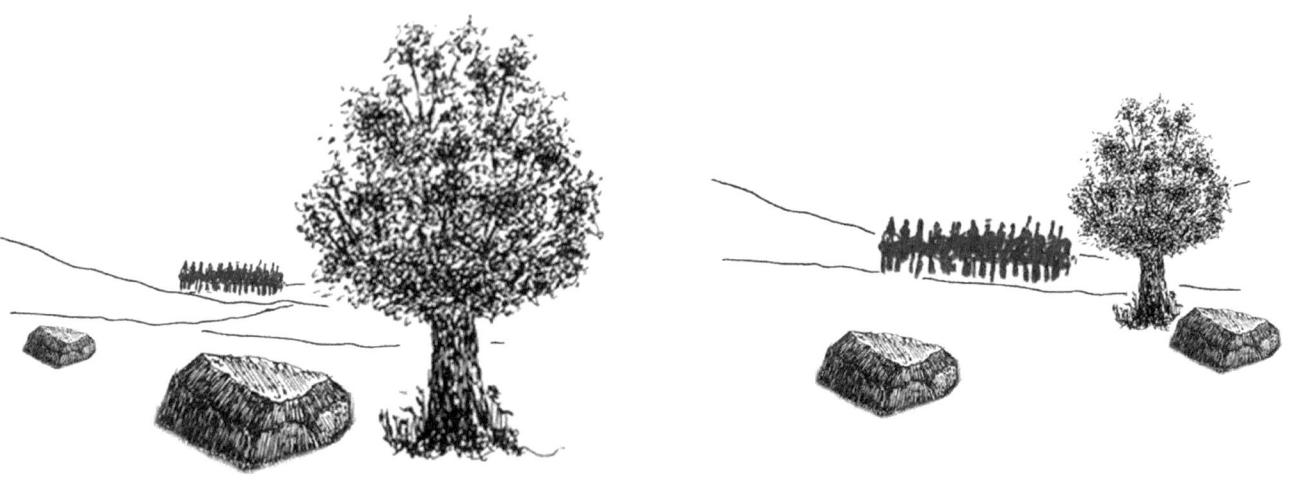

As the foreground stone and tree are moved to middle ground, they are reduced in size. Bringing the middle ground stone and background foliage closer also increases their size. The tree line is now in middle ground with implied background.

Relative Size of Middle Ground:

Space between background and foreground is considered middle ground. Depending on the size of drawing and your composition, it can be made bigger or smaller. If you have a path leading to the distant horizon, then a path leading over bigger middle ground to the distance is more appealing. On the other hand, if you are mainly focusing on the foreground, then to take away the attention from middle ground, it can be made smaller. Key point to understand is that more space for a ground gives it prominence and there should be something interesting on it to catch viewers attention.

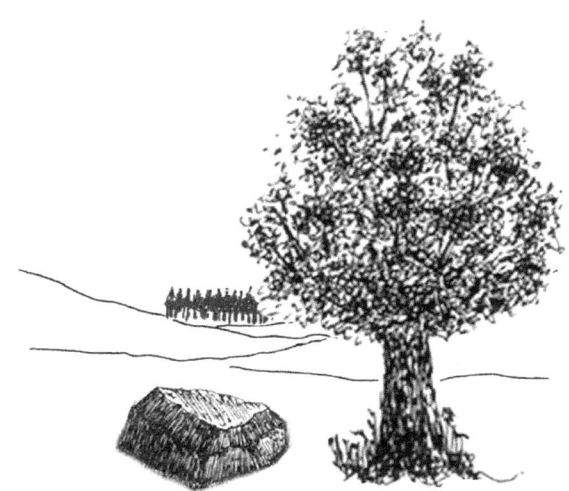

Smaller middle ground. Eyes quickly travel from foreground to background.

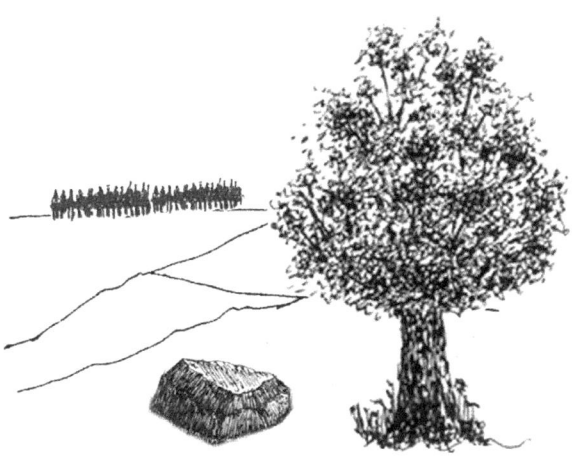

More space for middle ground. Without anything on it, it currently lacks interest.

Hidden Grounds:

Not all grounds need to be visible. If you are focusing on foreground, then elements on it might cover the view of other grounds. In the case, the other grounds are implied.

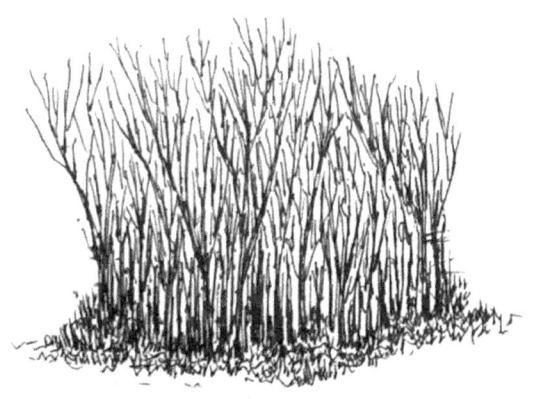

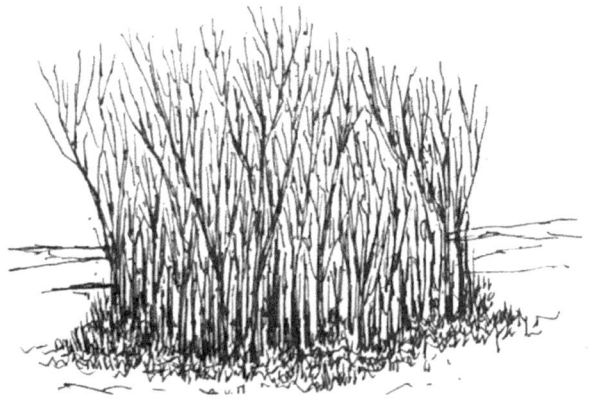

With no plain lines, middle ground and background are implied here.

Plain lines are added to the sides to give more visual indication of middle and background.

Interactive Plain Addition:

New plain lines can be added to create new foreground and other plains interactively. In the following drawing to left, winter bush is in the foreground. New foreground plains are further added to push winter bush to middle ground with stones and pine trees now in the foreground.

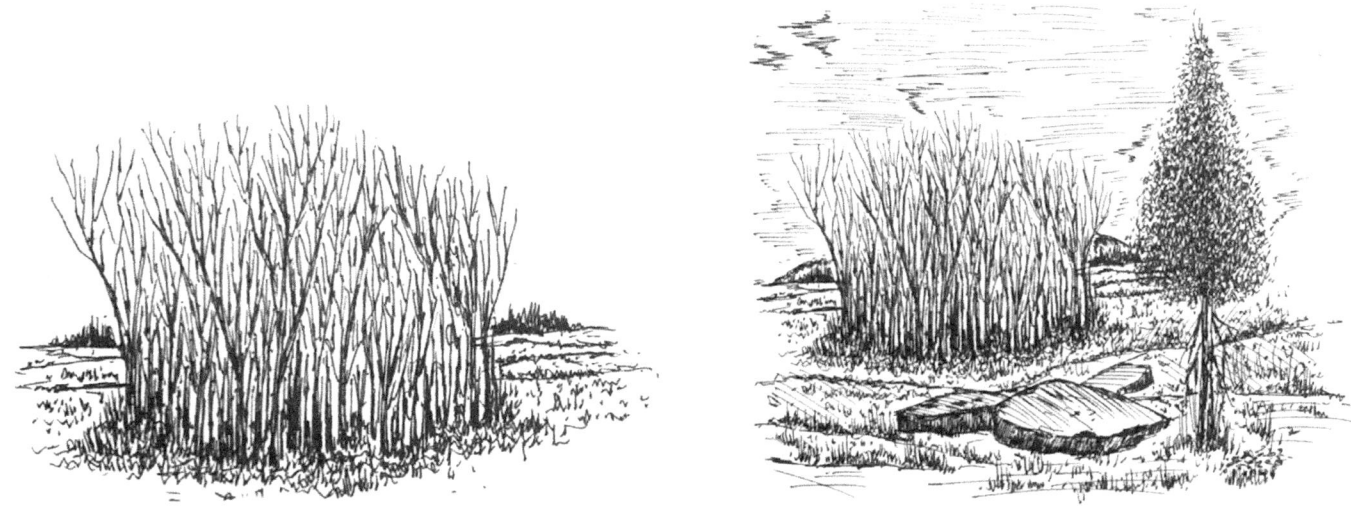

Adding new foreground plain here pushed earlier foreground to the middle ground. Interactively add such plain to your drawings to evolve them per your taste.

Step 2: Drawing Ground Contours:

After plains are drawn, next step is to indicate their surface contour. This further helps to bring out the form of the plains. In pen and ink, curved lines that are parallel to each other are used to define the contours of the surface. Curvature of lines indicate the curvature of the surface. Add such contour lines to define the contour of the plains and hence the ground . This should match orientation of the plain per its plain lines.

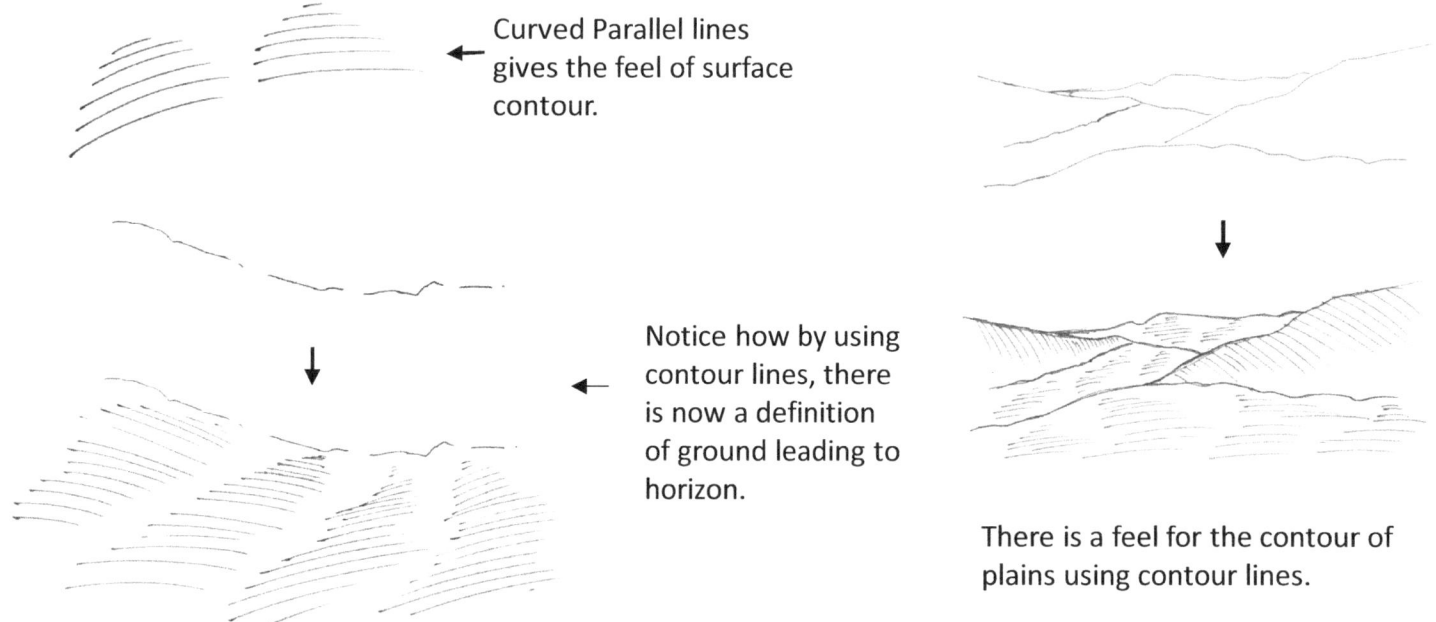

Curved Parallel lines gives the feel of surface contour.

Notice how by using contour lines, there is now a definition of ground leading to horizon.

There is a feel for the contour of plains using contour lines.

Drawing Contour Lines for Horizontal Plains:

For horizontal plains, the contour lines should be drawn along the plain with change in angle per the change in angle of plain line. Draw contour lines where there is a discernable change in angle of plain line.

Make contour lines bigger towards the viewer and make them smaller as it goes to horizon. This reinforces the distance and perspective.

Some white can be left between different set of contour lines to give it clean appearance.

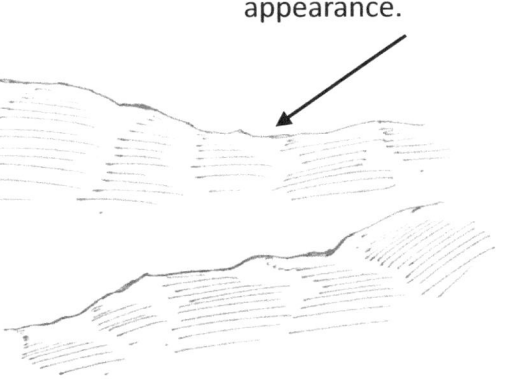

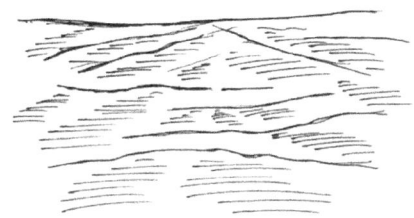

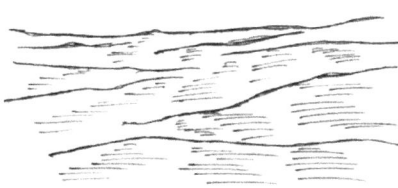

Notice how contour lines are reinforcing the distance and direction of plains.

Drawing Contour Lines for Angled Plains:

For angled plains, the contour lines should be drawn as shown below to bring out the curved form of the ground.

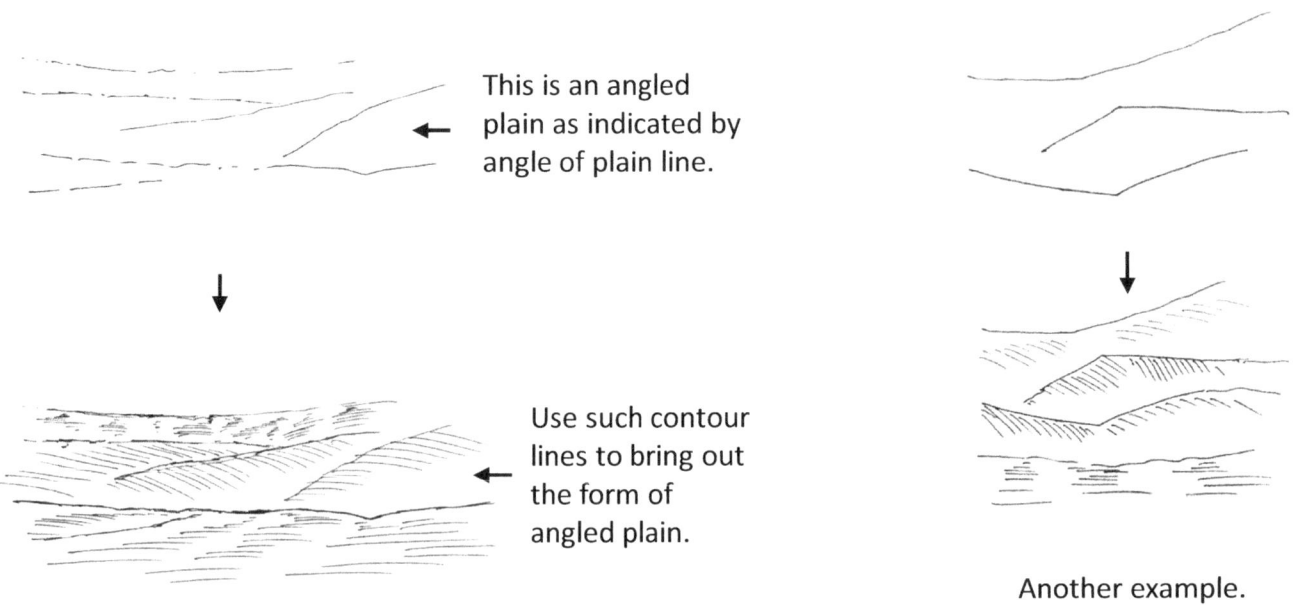

This is an angled plain as indicated by angle of plain line.

Use such contour lines to bring out the form of angled plain.

Another example.

Avoid Overlapping Contour Lines:

Any overlap in contour lines is usually unpleasing. Use shorter lines at transition points as shown below to avoid the overlap.

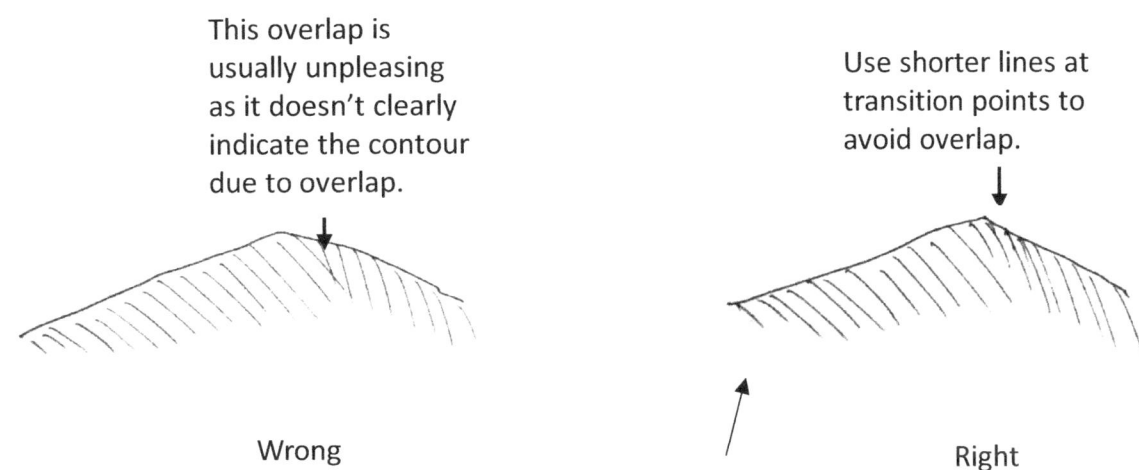

This overlap is usually unpleasing as it doesn't clearly indicate the contour due to overlap.

Use shorter lines at transition points to avoid overlap.

Wrong

Right

Taper the length of contour lines. Start small, draw progressively bigger till the middle of plain and then make it progressively smaller.

Appropriate Ground Contour Lines to Use:

Horizontal contour lines indicate flatness where as angled contour lines bring out the form of the plain. For plains with small angles both can be used as shown below based on desired effect.

Horizontal contour lines can still be use on horizontal plain lines with slight waviness.

↓

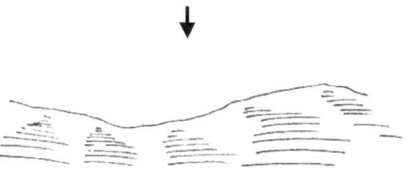

On the same plain line, using angled contour lines gives emphasis to its rounded form.

↓

Horizontal contour lines gives a feel of flatness.

Angled contour lines brings out the angular nature of plain.

Other Considerations for Ground Contour Lines:

Keep in mind following considerations when drawing contour lines. Lot of this comes with practice. Drawing interesting ground plains with contour lines is very fun to do and can be attempted in your short breaks.

For plains with high angular contour, horizontal lines looks odd.

↓

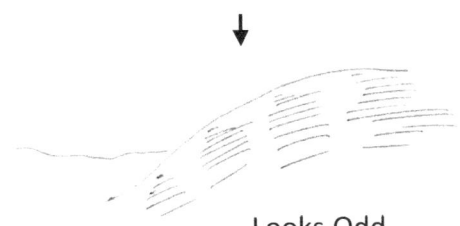

Looks Odd.

With smaller plains, avoid contour lines as it looks messy.

↓

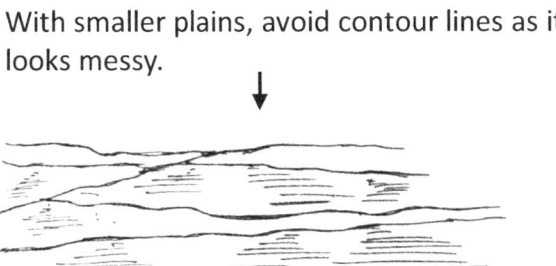

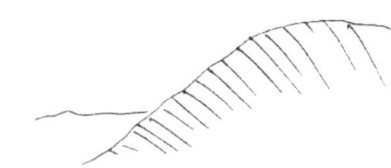

Angular Contour Lines works better.

Plains tend to become smaller and closer together as they go towards the horizon.

Help, I Can't Do Parallel Lines:

Drawing parallel lines, called 'hatching', is a fundamental technique in pen and ink drawing. It is very important to practice and get comfortable doing it. That said, if you are not currently comfortable with it, then following approach can be used.

Use dotted lines to lay down initial contour lines.

Connect dotes to create contour lines. They are not as clean as when drawing directly.

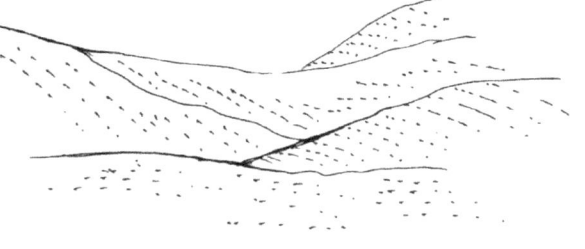

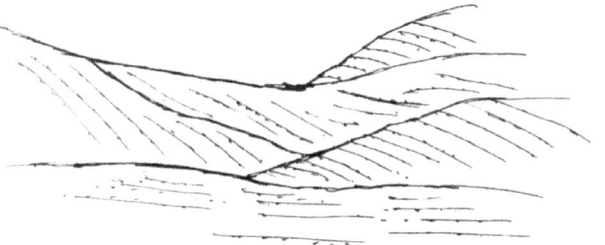

Activity: Drawing Surface Contours:

Practice drawing surface contours for the plain lines below. It takes time and practice. Carry a small pocket sketch book with you and practice drawing them when ever you get some time.

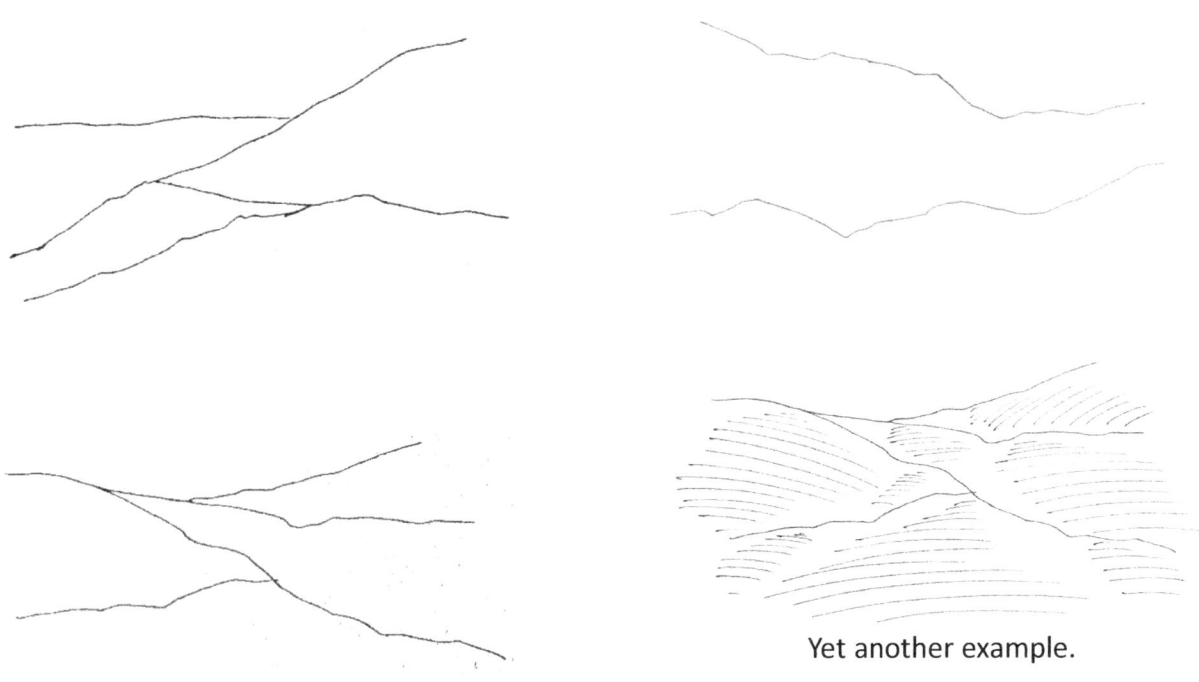

Yet another example.

With and Without Surface Contours:

As you can see below, adding surface contours really brings out the definition of ground and makes the drawing more interesting.

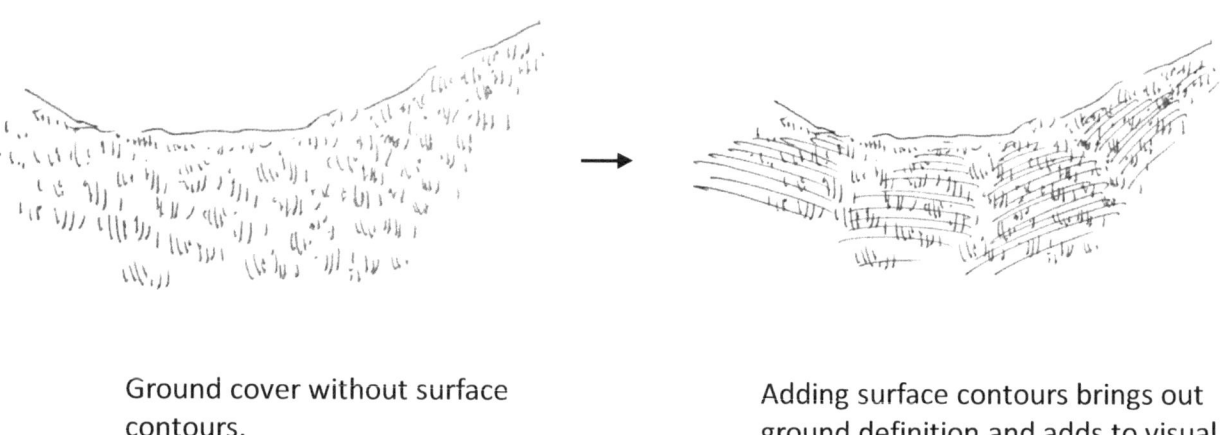

Ground cover without surface contours.

Adding surface contours brings out ground definition and adds to visual interest.

Step 3: Adding Ground Cover:

Next step is to give indication of ground cover/grass using following stroke. Notice how with just few grass strokes on surface contour lines, a pleasing feel of ground is conveyed.

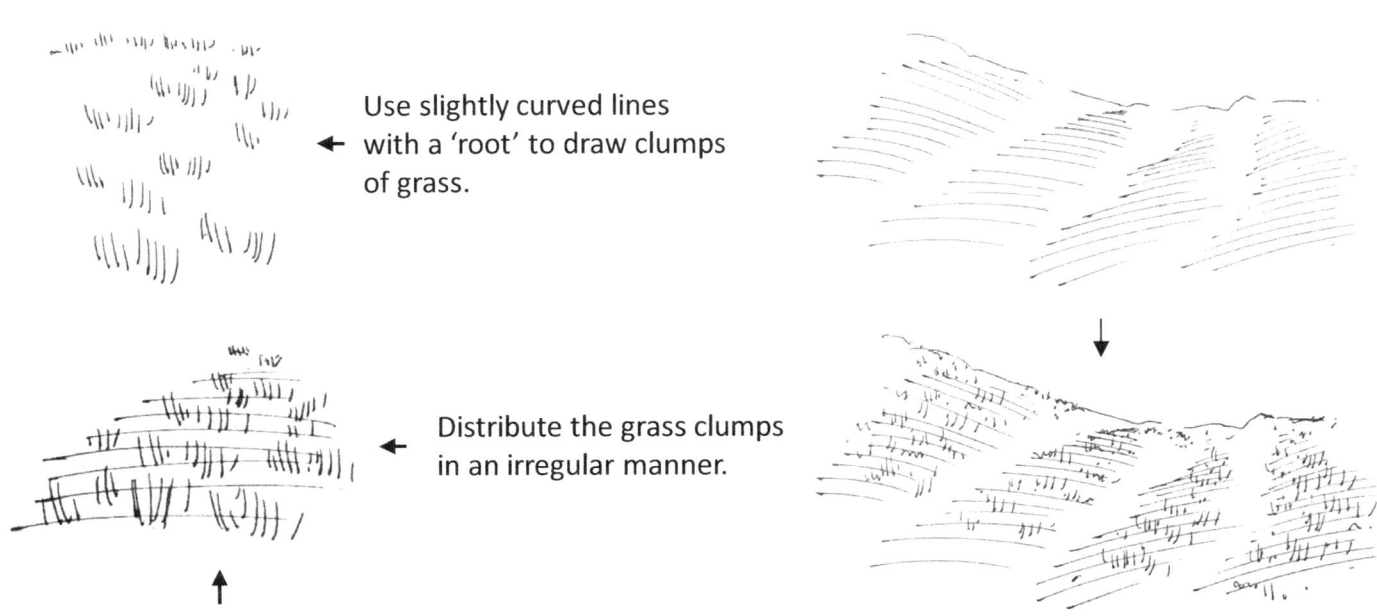

← Use slightly curved lines with a 'root' to draw clumps of grass.

← Distribute the grass clumps in an irregular manner.

↑ Size of grass increases as it goes towards the Viewer.

Addition of grass completes the ground.

Close-up of Ground Cover Stroke:

Study the grass stroke in detail below. For far away plains closer to horizon, indicate ground cover with few dots and wiggles. Increase the size and density of grass as plains get closer to viewer/foreground. In foreground, clump of flowers and other foliage can be added as well.

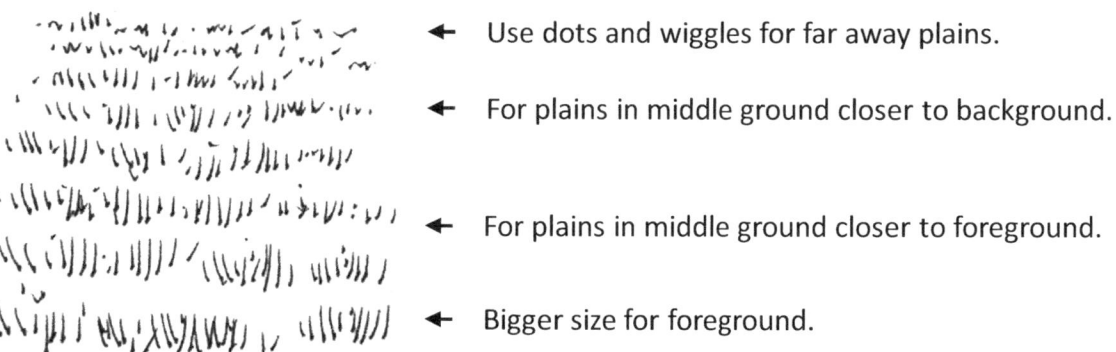

← Use dots and wiggles for far away plains.

← For plains in middle ground closer to background.

← For plains in middle ground closer to foreground.

← Bigger size for foreground.

Some More Examples of Adding Ground Cover:

Below are some more examples of adding ground cover to contour lines drawn earlier. Notice how a pleasant feel of ground is obtained just by drawing surface contours and grass on it.

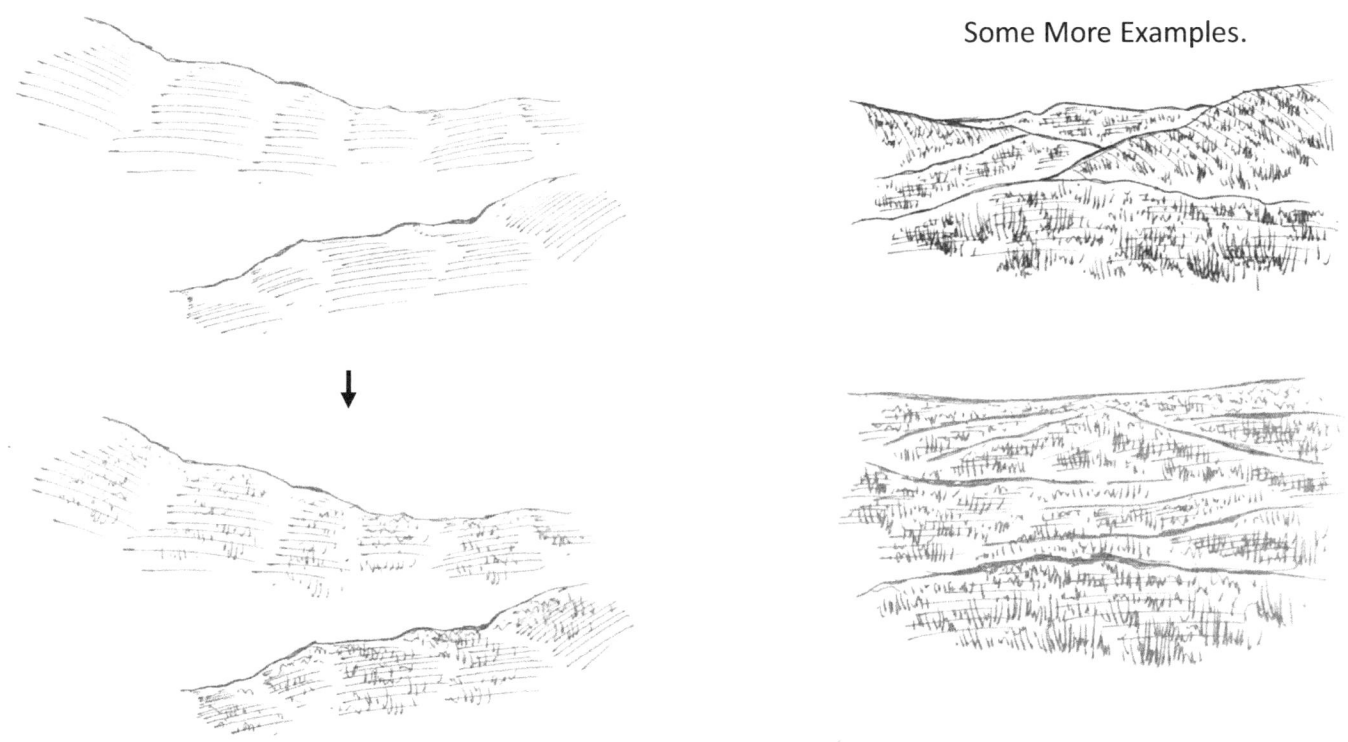

Some More Examples.

Yet More Examples:

Following are some more examples to study. Notice how contour lines are visible under the grass and provide sense of form of the plain.

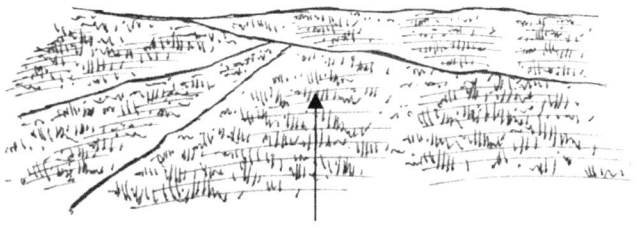

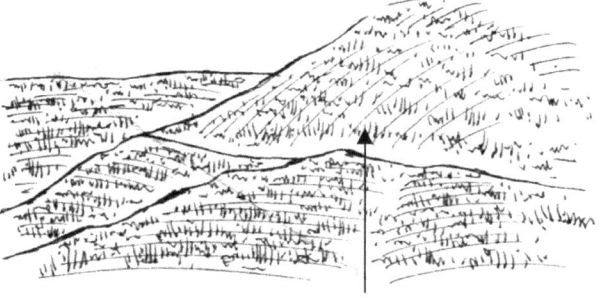

For horizontal plains, use grass to reinforce distance by tapering them per the contour lines.

Angular plains receives more light on the top and are brighter there. Use less stroke on the top and more towards the bottom to bring out that feel.

Relative Intensity of Ground Cover:

Relative intensity of ground cover can be varied by changing density of grass cover used. Lighter ground cover contrasts well with the darker tone of distant tree line as we will see next but darker ground cover can be used for more emphasis if desired.

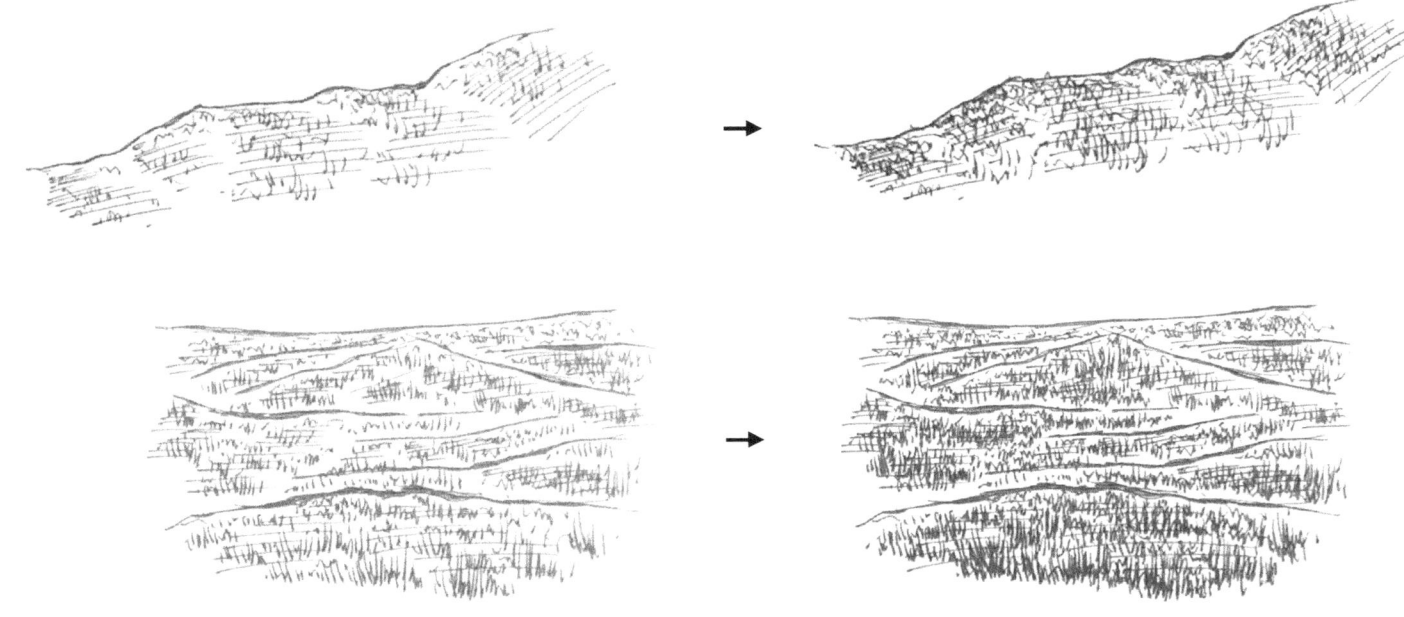

Add more stroke to increase the tone.

Variation in Intensity of Ground Cover:

Instead of just light or dark, add variation in intensity of ground cover to make it visually interesting as shown below. As we will see in detail later, tonal intensity of other elements on ground will also dictate the right tone to use for ground cover.

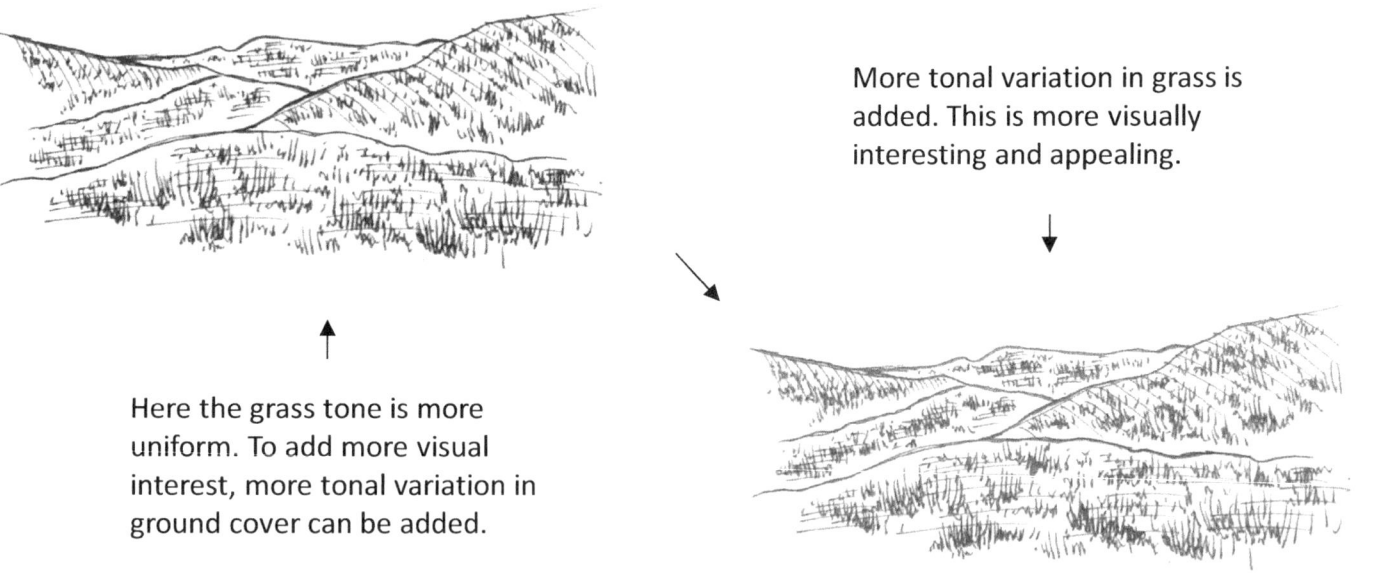

More tonal variation in grass is added. This is more visually interesting and appealing.

Here the grass tone is more uniform. To add more visual interest, more tonal variation in ground cover can be added.

Use Contrast in Ground Cover To Add Interest:

Following is another example of use of tonal variation in grass cover to add more visual interest. Darker spots surrounded by lighter areas acts a focal points in a drawing and attracts viewers interest. By selectively creating such focal points by using different intensity of ground cover, more interest can be added in a drawing. Remember to not over do it.

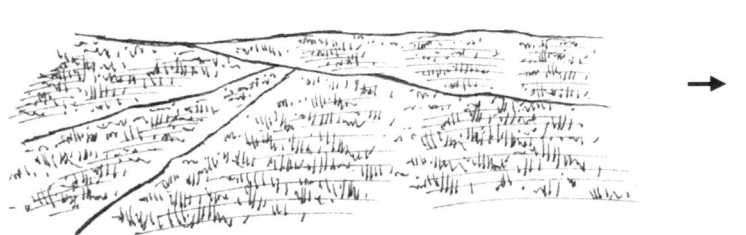 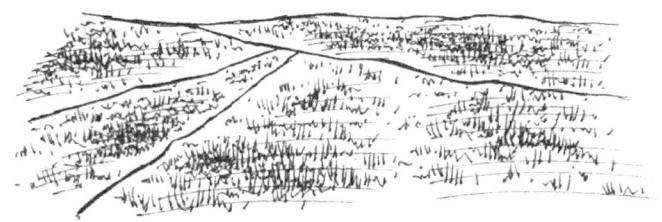

Ground cover has uniform tone. This will highlight other darker elements that are added to the ground (like trees, stones etc.)

Non uniform ground cover acts as focal point and makes this drawing interesting in of itself. Darker tone makes it difficult to add other elements on the ground.

Use Contrast in Ground Cover To Add Interest, Continued:

Darker ground cover makes it difficult to add other elements on it. Another approach is to add darker foliage to plain lines to create some focal points. Other darker elements can still be added on ground (away from plain lines). This approach is discussed in more detail later.

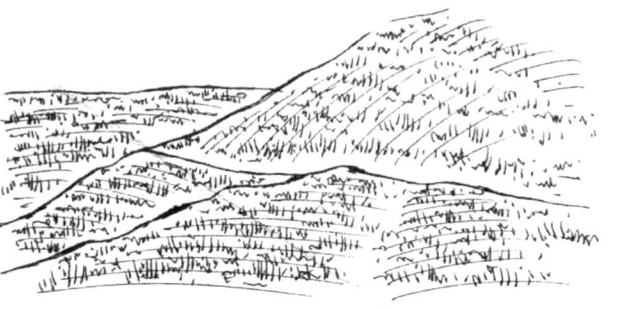 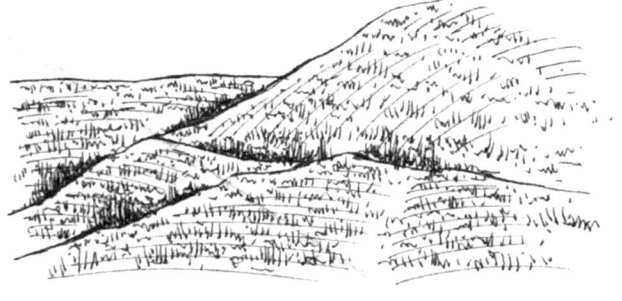

Uniform light tone in of itself is unattractive.

Add more grass stroke in a tapered manner to the plain lines. Keep it non uniform and interesting. Your eyes are attracted to these darker focal points. These also serve to distinguish and highlight plains.

Let Your Imagination Be The Guide:

Use of contrast to add visual interest in a drawing is a fundamental trait to learn. Lot of it comes with practice. Aim is to combine darker and lighter areas in interesting ways for viewers to be attracted to darker areas (focal points) in a fluid way across the drawing. Experiment with different tones for ground and other elements to ring out the desired effect in your drawing.

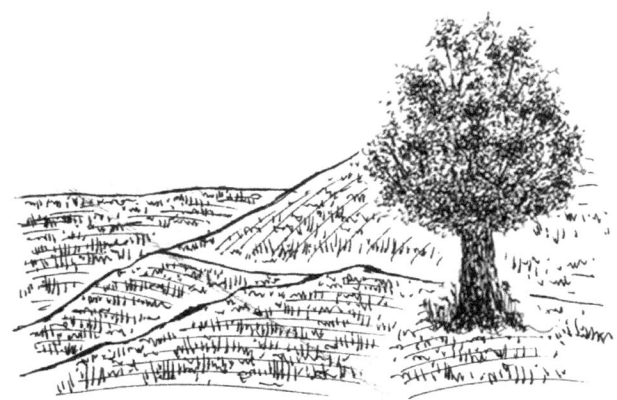

Against a lighter ground, darker tree acts as a focal point and provide viewing interest.

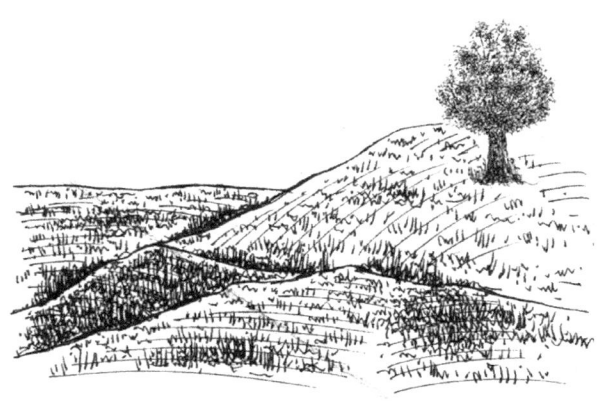

Ground tone is more varied here. Darker tree is used on lighter ground plain in a corner to attract viewer across the drawing.

Adding Flowers in Foreground:

If foreground is the main focus as in drawing below, then flowers and other type of ground cover can be added to make it more interesting. Leave some white around them for them to stand out.

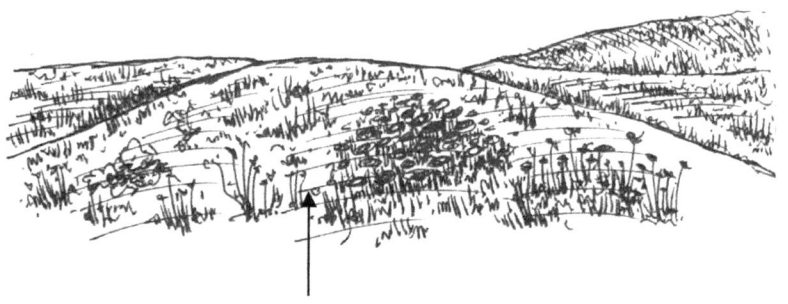

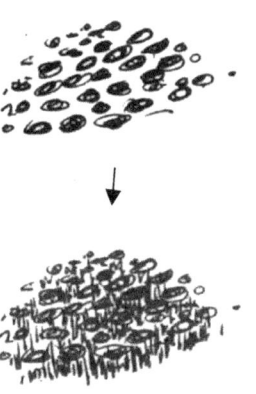

Such ground is more appealing than just grass. Some white is left around cluster of flowers for them to stand out. This is necessary in pen and ink where colors can't be used to distinguish elements.

To draw ground covered with flower, draw dark ovals representing flowers in irregular manner. Use lines next to indicate their stem.

Activity: Drawing Ground Cover:

Practice drawing ground cover on the following contour lines. Add ground cover also to contour lines you drew earlier.

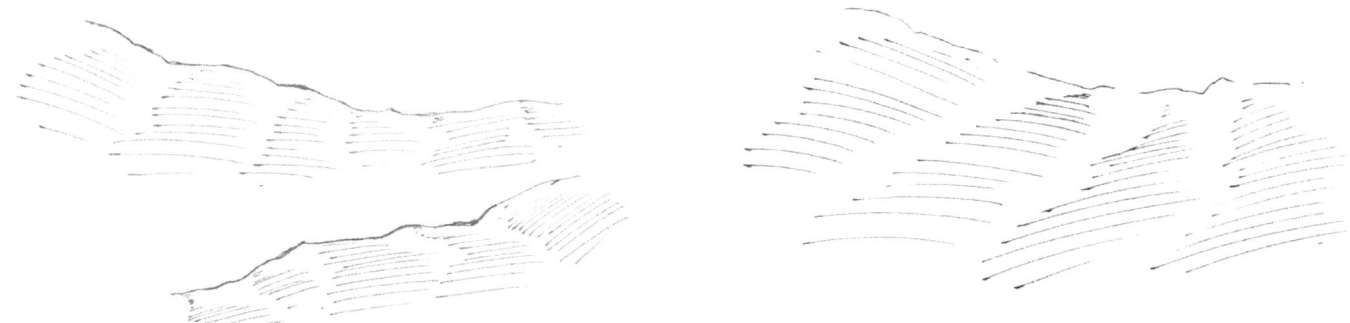

Additional Techniques for Texturing Ground:

Ground can be textured in many other ways and 3 additional techniques are discussed later. Different techniques provide different feel for the ground and can even be combined as seen later. You can learn these additional techniques now or go on to the next step.

Technique described on page 144

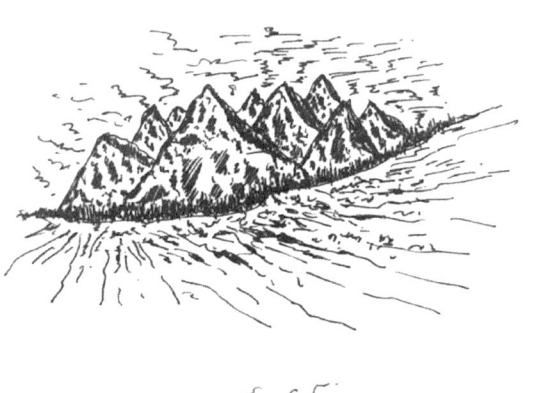

Technique described on page 139

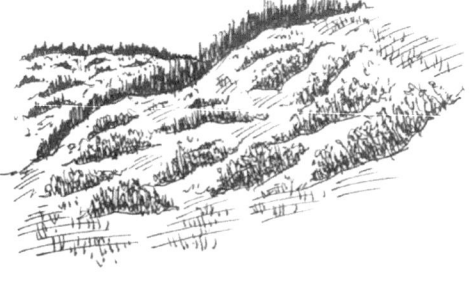

Technique described on page 146

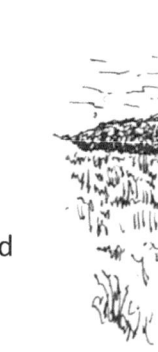

Step 4: Adding Distant Element on Horizon:

Next a distant element is added on the horizon line. As our eyes travel the foreground taking in the surface contours and ground cover, it rests on the distant element which is usually some kind of tree line.

Notice how addition of distant element creates a focal point with its darker tone and makes our eyes travel to it from the foreground. Such contrast between darker distant element and lighter foreground provides a pleasing contrast in the drawing.

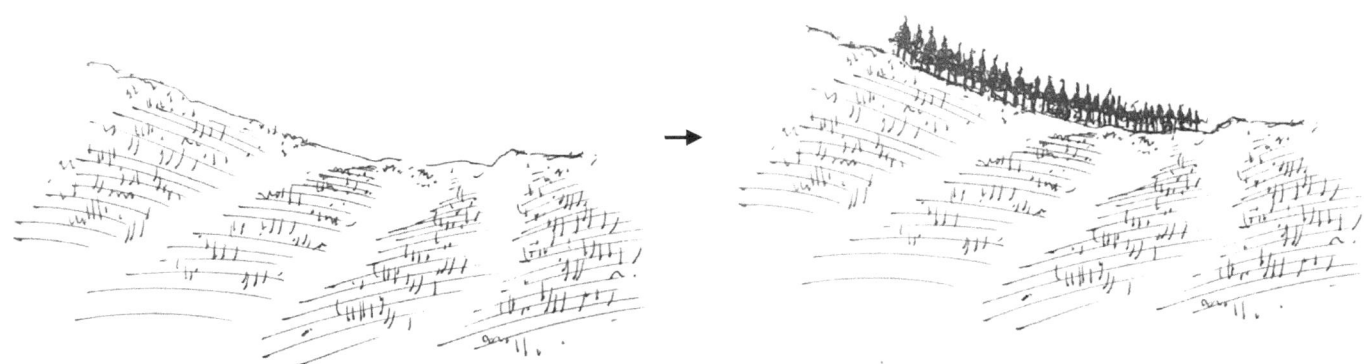

More Examples of Adding Distant Element:

Following are 2 earlier drawings to which distant element of a tree line has been added. The size of distant elements indicates to our mind their perceived distance.

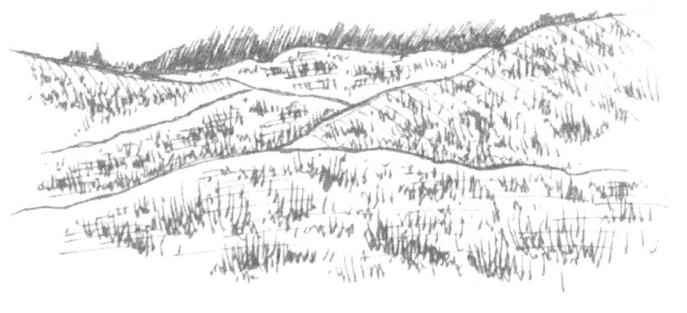

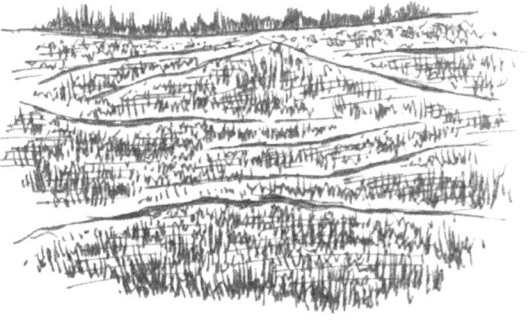

On a not too dark ground cover, distant element stands out as a focal point and draws our attention.

With a darker ground cover, distant element doesn't stand out as much.

Different Techniques for Drawing Distant Element:

There are many ways in which distant elements can be drawn. Following are some simple techniques.

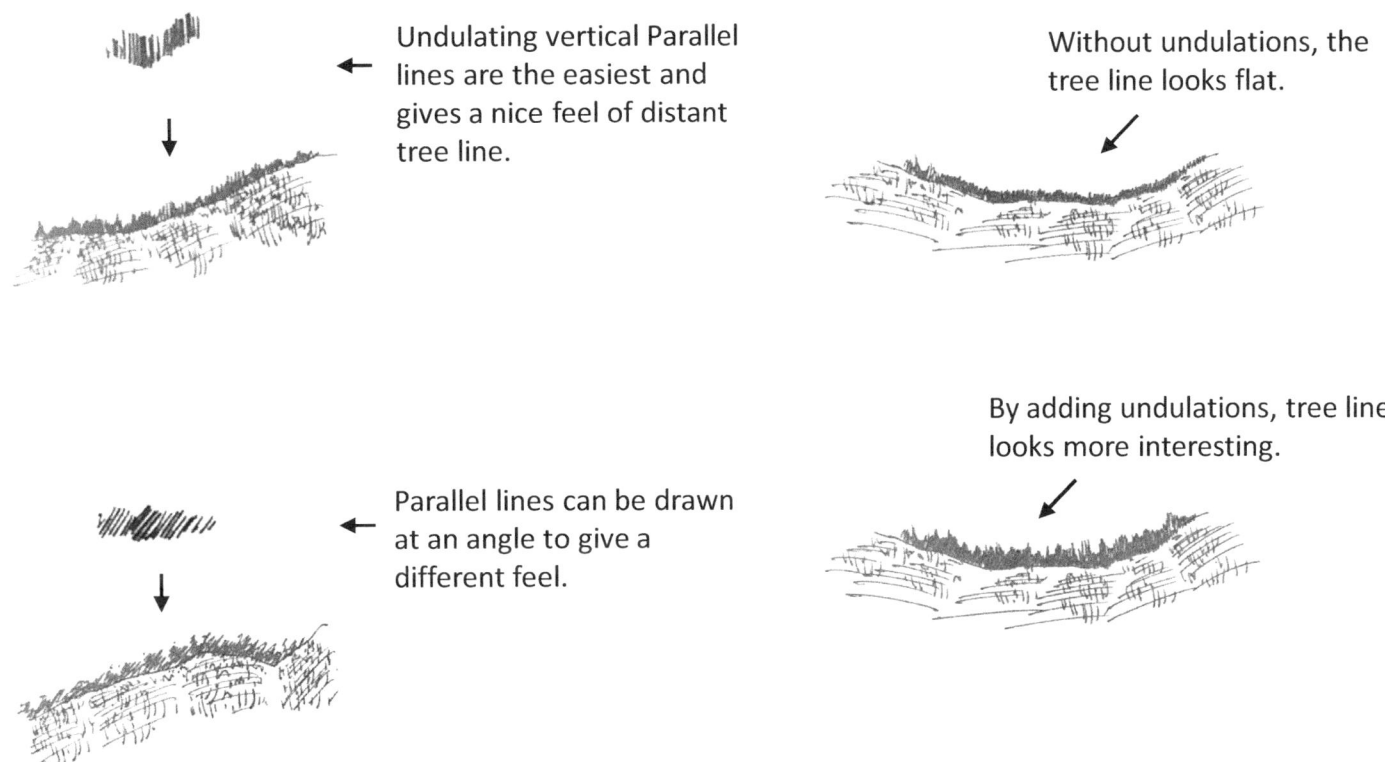

← Undulating vertical Parallel lines are the easiest and gives a nice feel of distant tree line.

Without undulations, the tree line looks flat.

By adding undulations, tree line looks more interesting.

← Parallel lines can be drawn at an angle to give a different feel.

Different Techniques for Drawing Distant Element, Continued:

Distant Pine Trees can be drawn using following simple steps.

Tapered tops gives an impression of pine trees as our brain is accustomed to it. Make sure such shape is clearly visible.

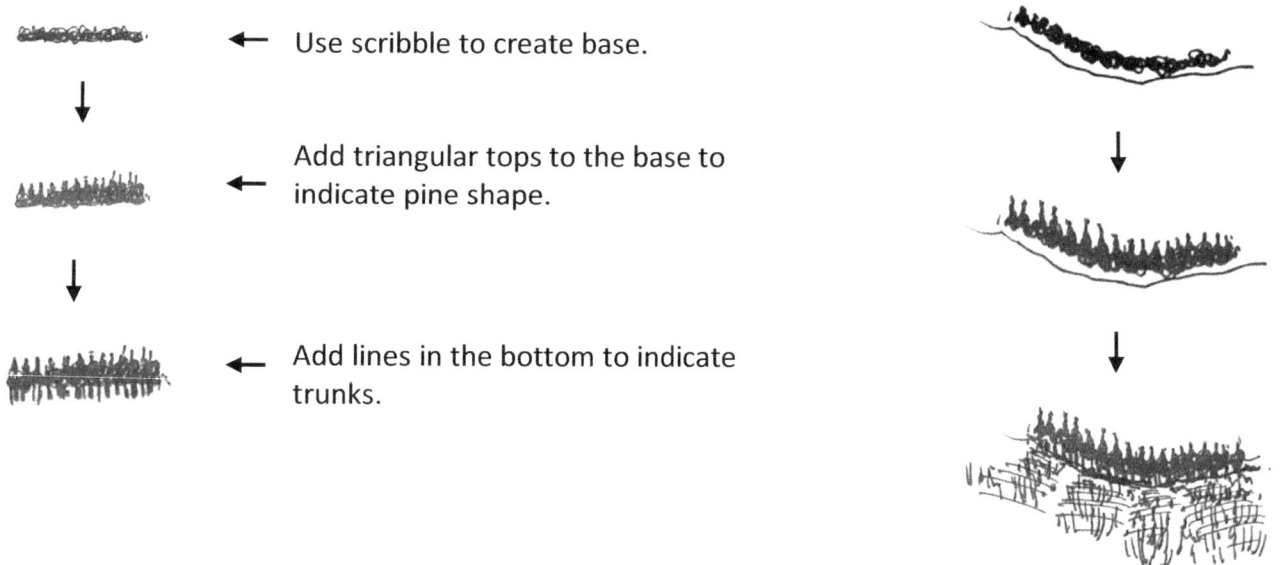

← Use scribble to create base.

← Add triangular tops to the base to indicate pine shape.

← Add lines in the bottom to indicate trunks.

Different Techniques for Drawing Distant Element, Continued:

Following are some additional techniques for drawing distant element.

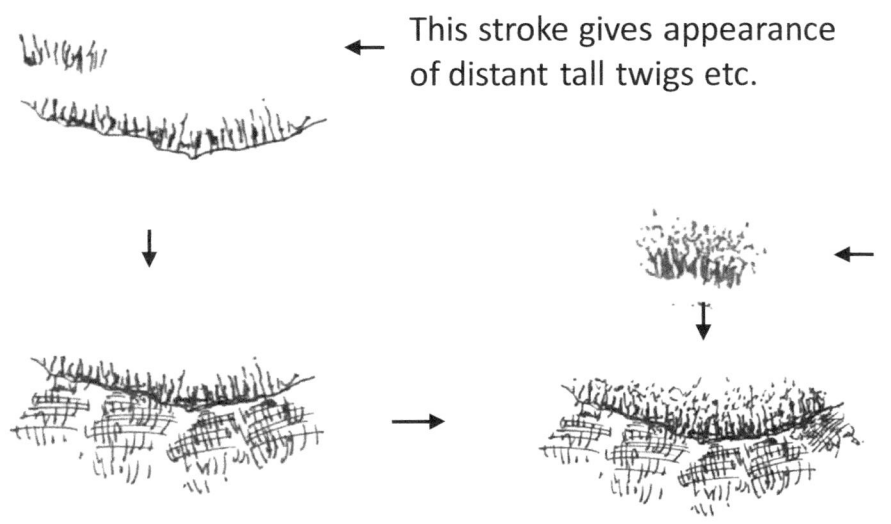

← This stroke gives appearance of distant tall twigs etc.

← Using small tick marks, a feel of foliage can be added as well. This gives appearance of distant bush.

Different Techniques for Drawing Distant Element, Continued:

Use following technique to draw a distant tree line with distinct trees shapes visible.

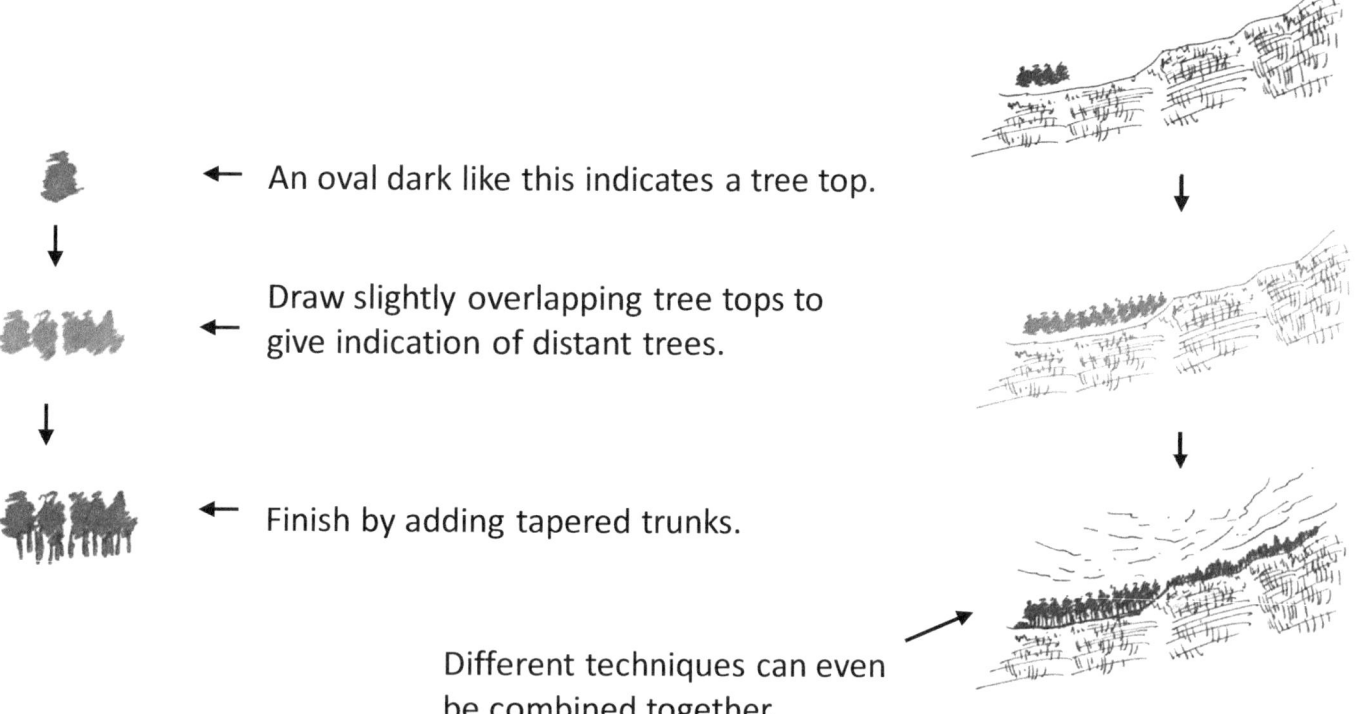

← An oval dark like this indicates a tree top.

← Draw slightly overlapping tree tops to give indication of distant trees.

← Finish by adding tapered trunks.

Different techniques can even be combined together.

Two Tone Distant Element for Adding Depth:

Following approach can be used to create layers of distant element. This adds to perception of depth.

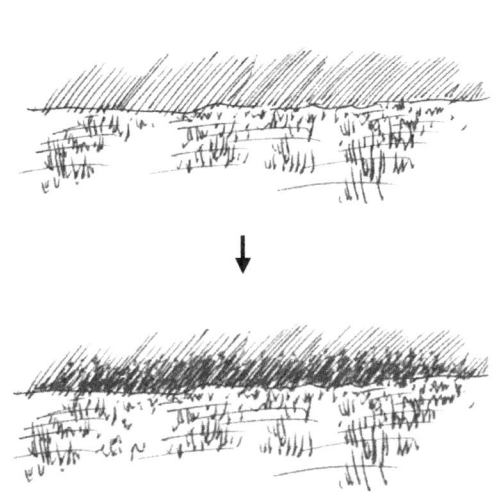

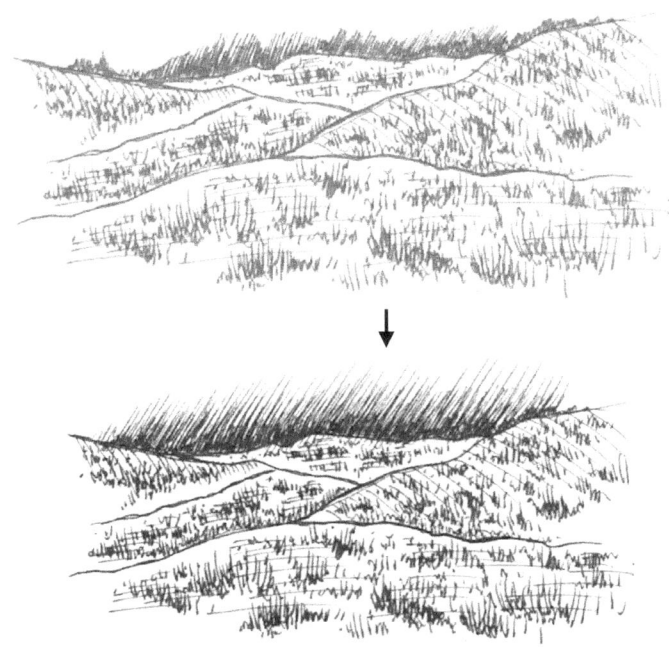

Start with a lighter tone for slightly larger first layer of angular parallel lines. Add darker smaller layer of distant element to create two tome distant element.

Multiple layers with different tones can be used as well for distant element.

Effect of Size of Distant Element:

As the size of distant element is increased, it is perceived to be closer to viewer due to perspective. Use the appropriate size based on how close or far you want it to be.

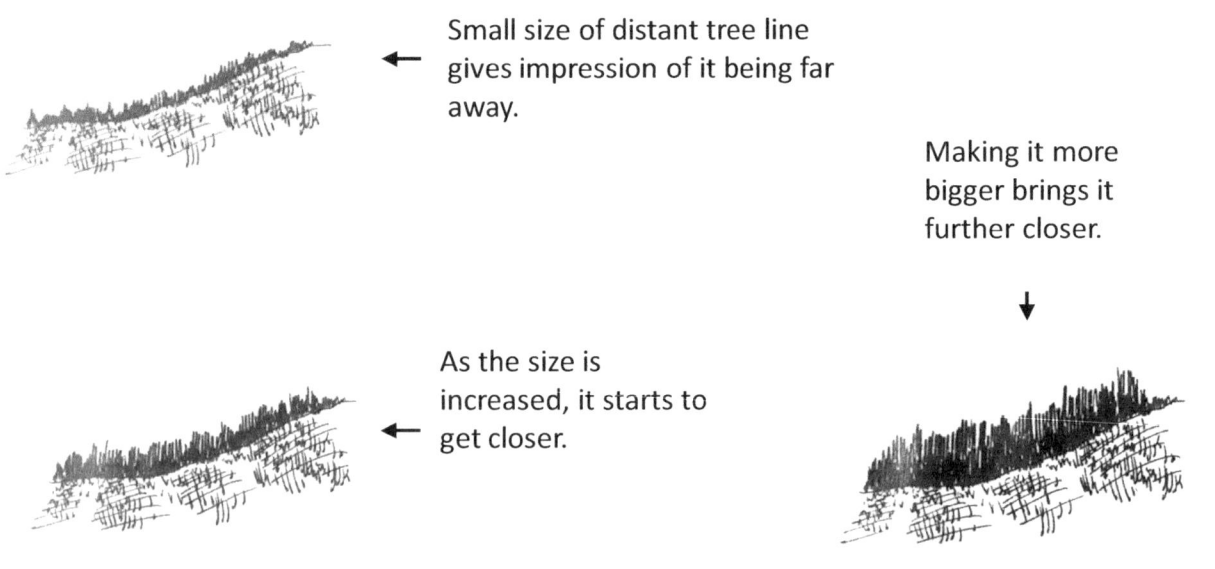

Small size of distant tree line gives impression of it being far away.

Making it more bigger brings it further closer.

As the size is increased, it starts to get closer.

Effect of Size of Distant Element, Continued:

Here is another example. As the size of distant element increases, it is brought closer to our mind (as we see closer things bigger). Draw distant element at a size that you want to indicate its closeness to the viewer.

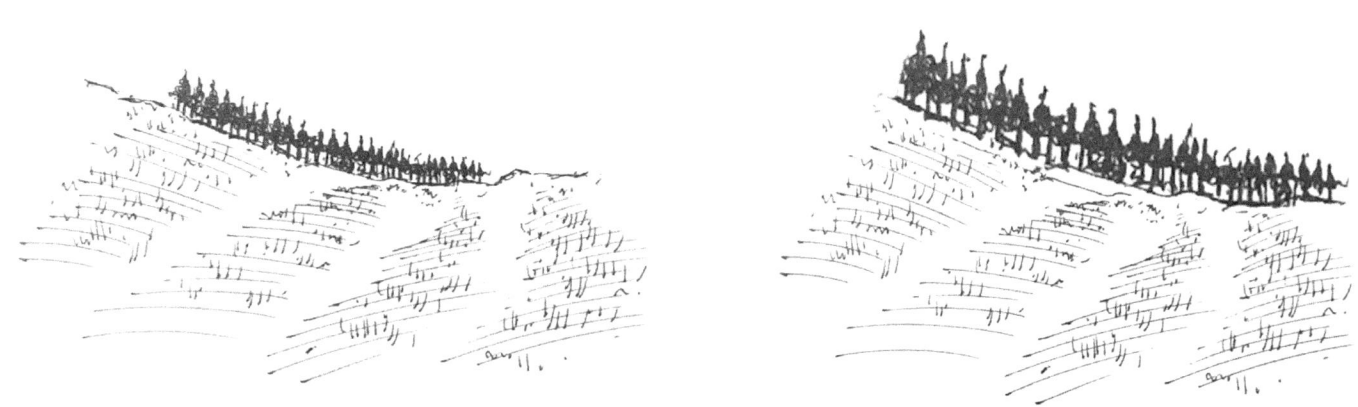

Smaller size of tree line indicates it is further out than one on right, where their size is bigger. Our mind adjusts the perceived distance of ground with the same ground indicating more or less distance based on size of distant element.

Keep Size Consistent With Distance:

In addition to horizon, 'Distant Element' can be added to other plains as well. In this case, keep the size of distant element consistent across plains with bigger size for closer plains and progressively smaller size for distant plains. This reinforces the feel of distance per perspective.

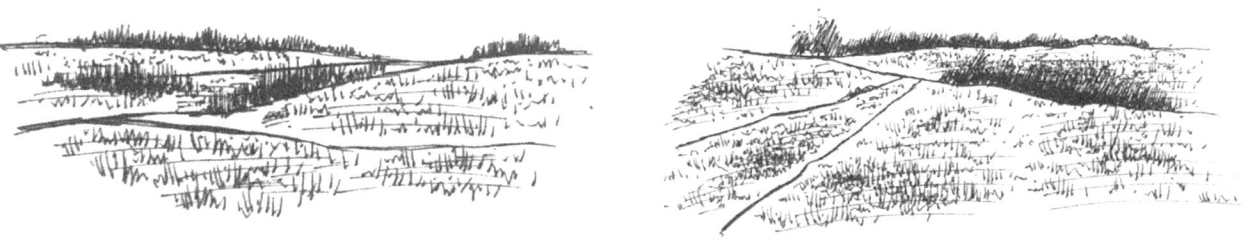

Distant elements/foliage is drawn bigger on plains closer to viewer and made progressively smaller as it goes out. This reinforces the feel of distance to our mind.

Activity: Drawing Distant Element:

Practice drawing distant element in following drawings and ones you completed earlier. Try different techniques discussed earlier with different sizes. Supplement it with practice in your own sketch book.

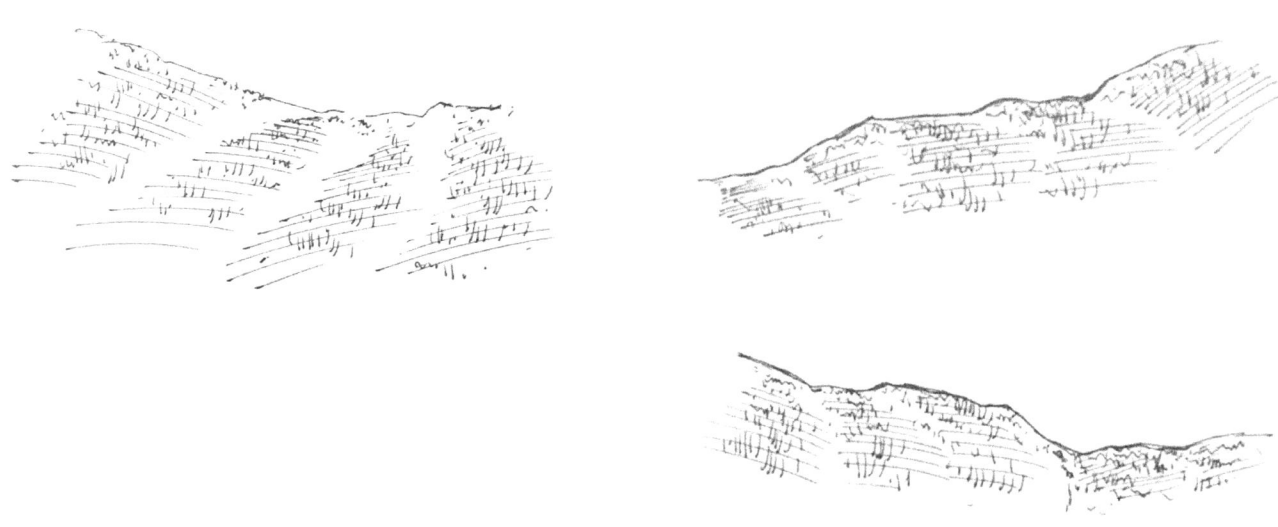

Step 5: Adding Background Element:

As a final step, a distant hill or mountains can be drawn behind the distant tree line to add interest in the drawing. This creates a nice composition where our eyes takes in the contours of foreground surface while travelling to distant tree line and then enjoys the backdrop of hills before resting there. Sky/Clouds aren't added here but can be done so as well.

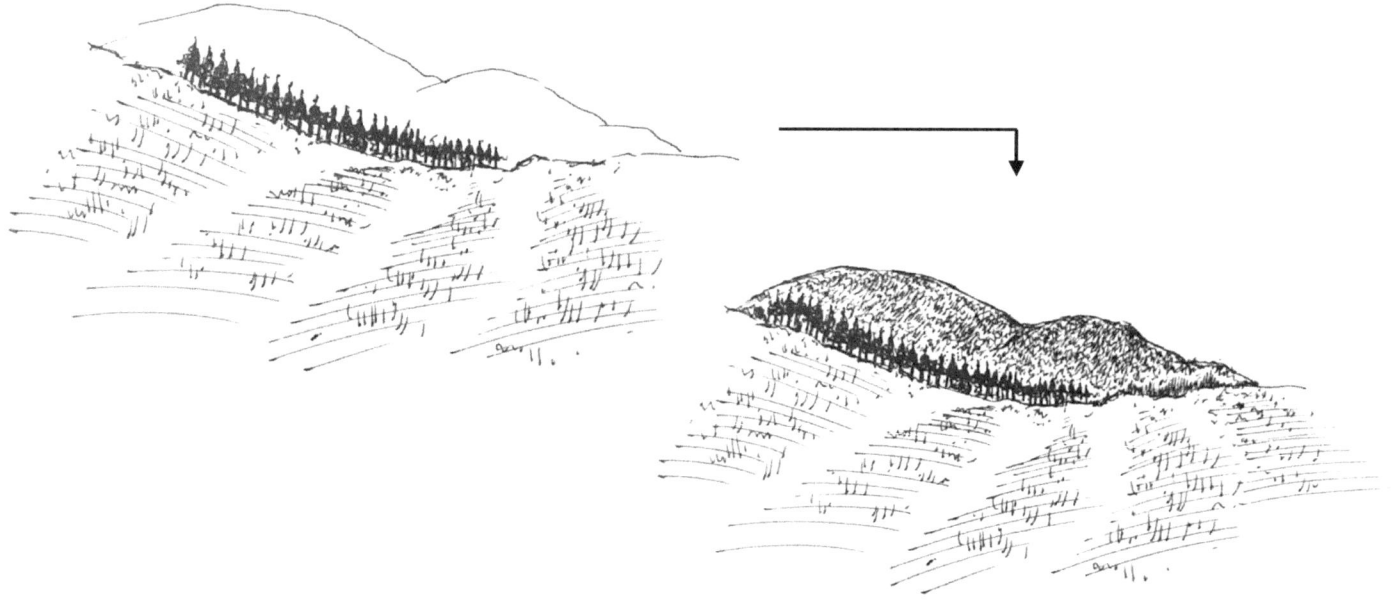

Drawing a Distant Hill:

To draw a distant hill, use short angular lines as shown below. These are similar to what we used to create distant element earlier. A distant hill can be given lighter or darker tone by using different density of stroke.

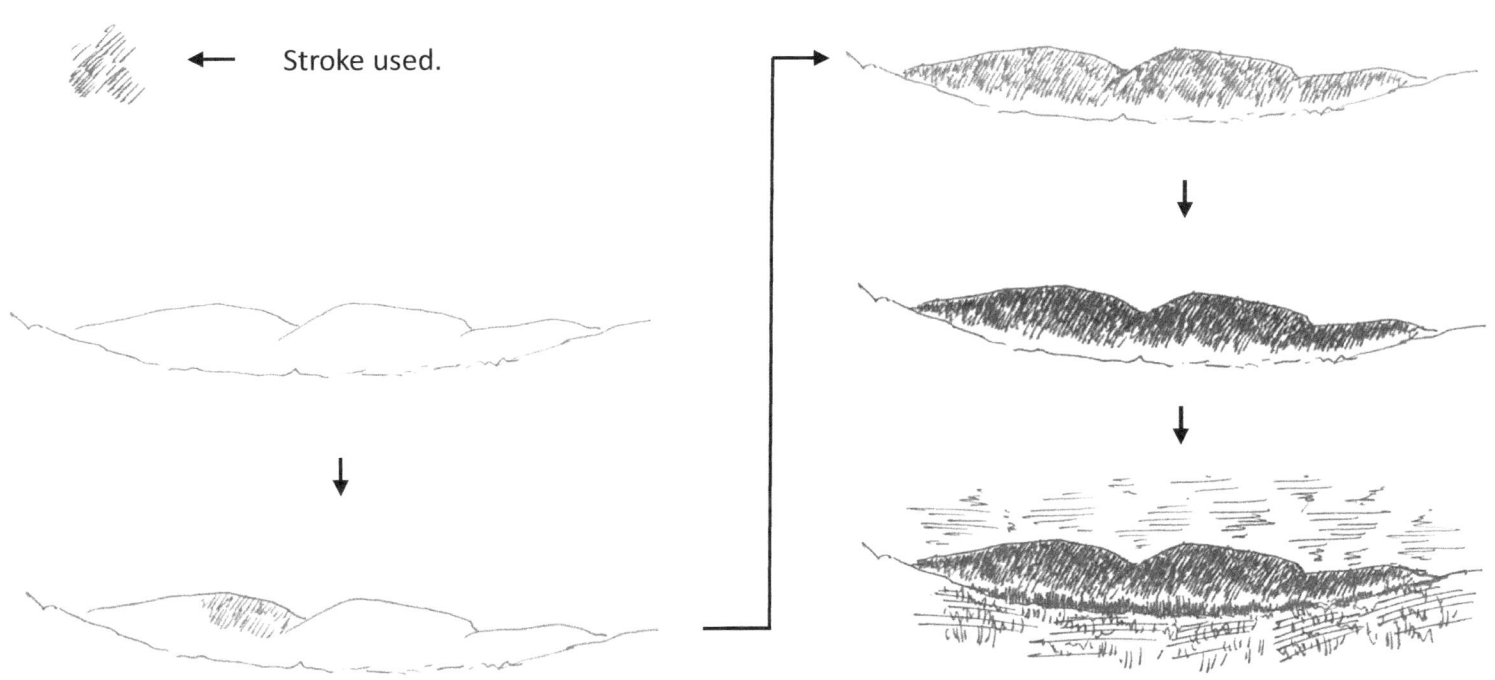

Drawing a Distant Hill, Continued:

Here is an alternate stroke to use for drawing distant hill. The stroke consists of combination of small ticks and dots.

Any combination of such small ticks, dots, small angular lines etc. can be used to texture distant hills.

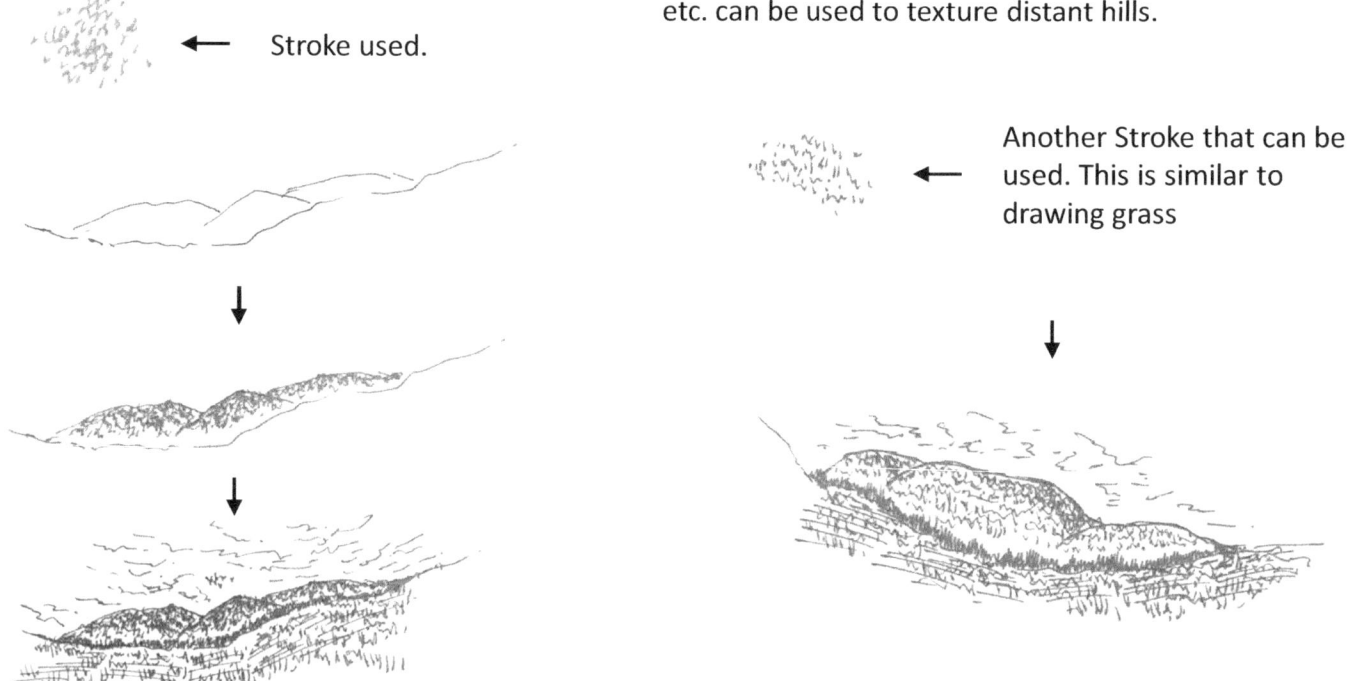

← Stroke used.

← Another Stroke that can be used. This is similar to drawing grass

Use of Different Tones:

Different level of tones used for hills gives different feel to them. Darker tone gives a more heavier feel where as lighter tone make then feel more sunlit. Experiment with different level of tones to see what you prefer.

Some of the drawings we saw earlier that use different tones for hills.

Notice the difference in feel of the hill as its tone is darkened.

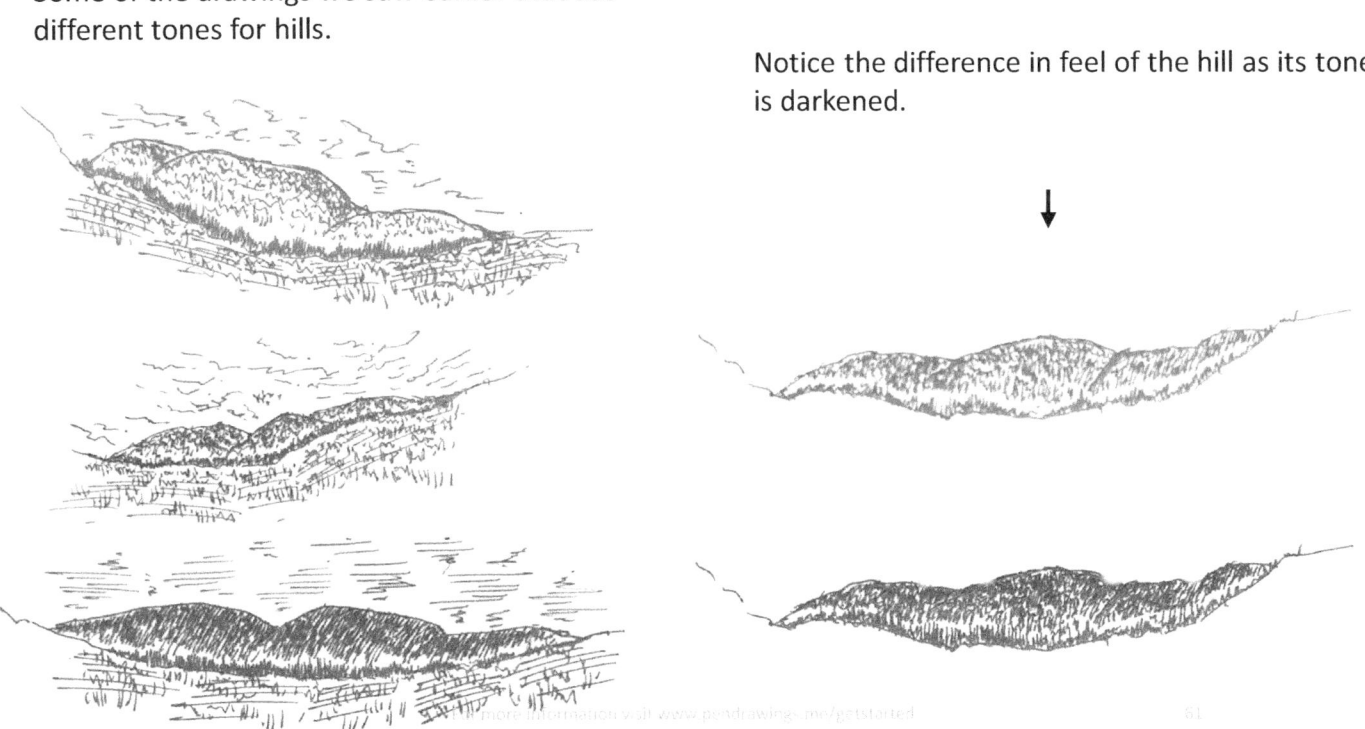

Activity: Drawing Distant Hills:

Practice texturing distant hills in the outline below. Draw some of your own.

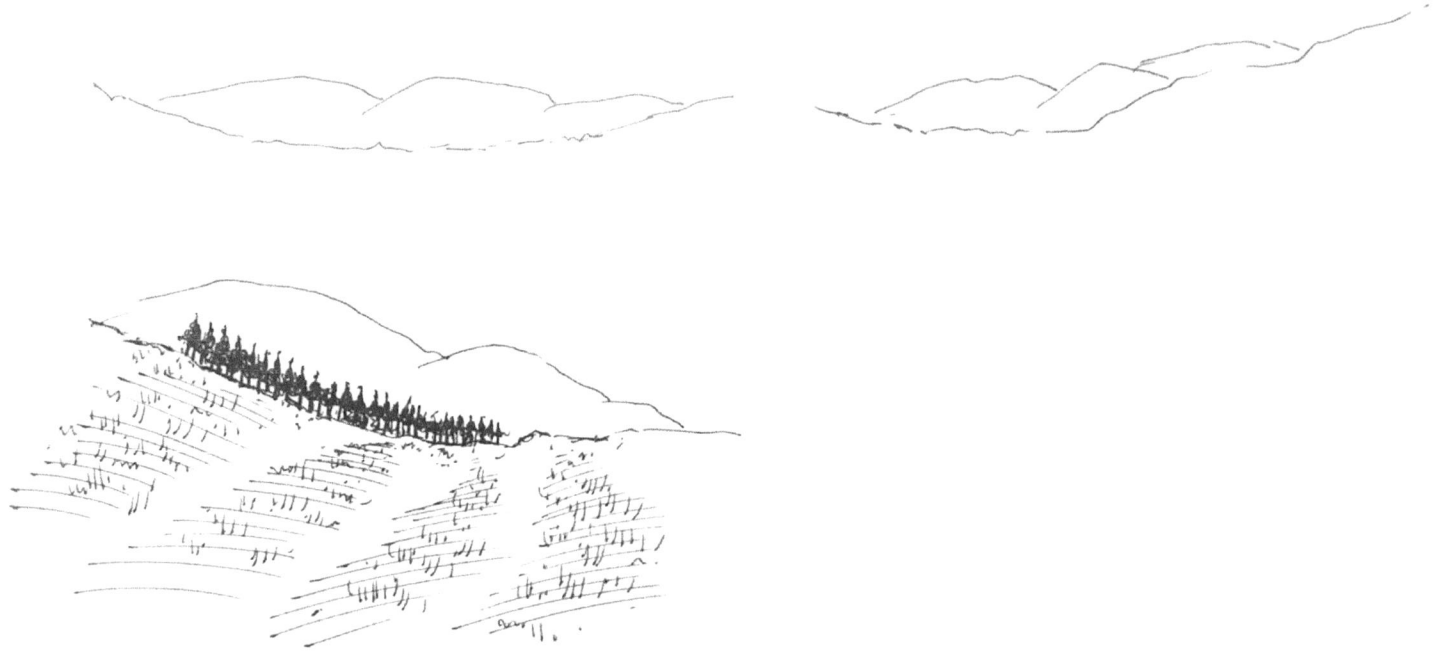

Drawing a Range of Hills:

Receding range of hills adds further interest to the drawing and makes them more appealing. The key point is to make the base of hills in the back darker and top lighter so that they stand apart from each other.

Darken the base of hill behind while leaving top lighter. This serves to bring out form and also distinguish between successive layers. Make successive layers smaller.

Behind hill can also be darkened to make it a focal point and draw interest to it

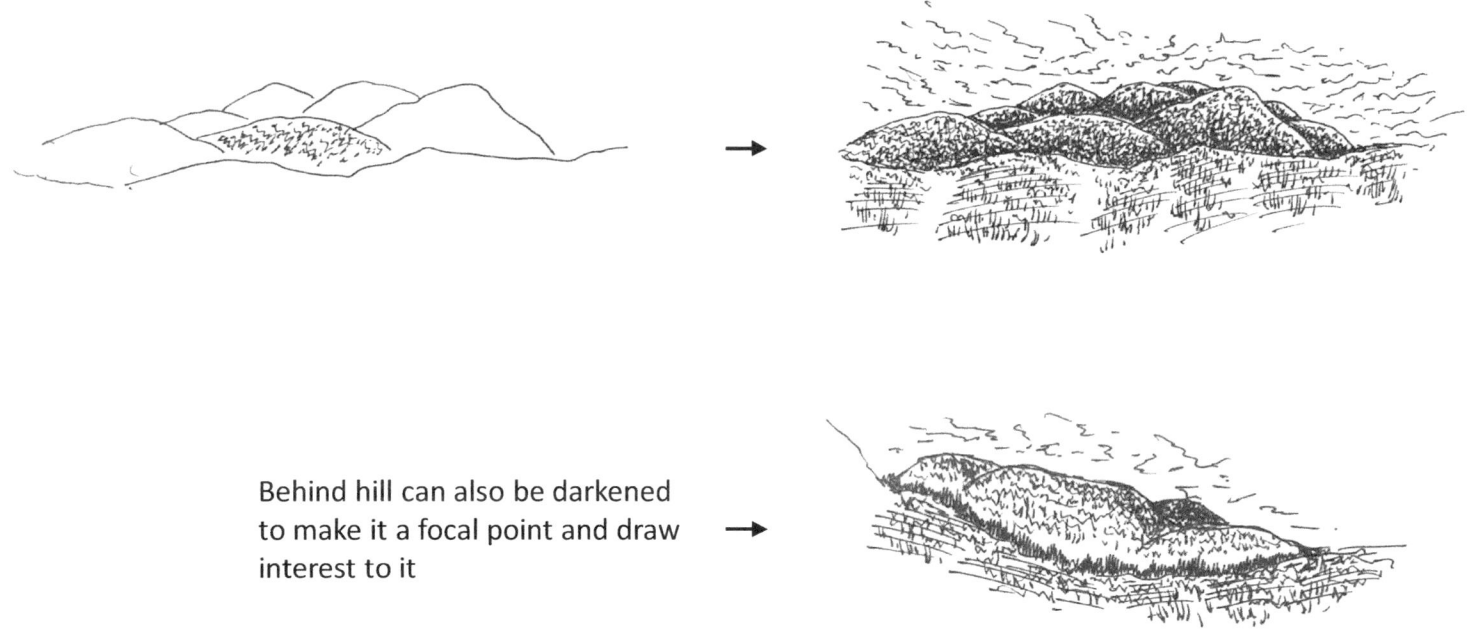

Importance of Leaving White:

In the absence of color, to differentiate between adjacent elements in a pen and ink drawing, there either has to be a distinct change in tone from one element to another or a small sliver of white should be left between them for them to stand out.

When darker tone is used for the hills, leaving small white between them makes them stand apart.

Small white is left between distant tree line and base of hill for them to stand apart. Same is also done between distant tree line and ground cover

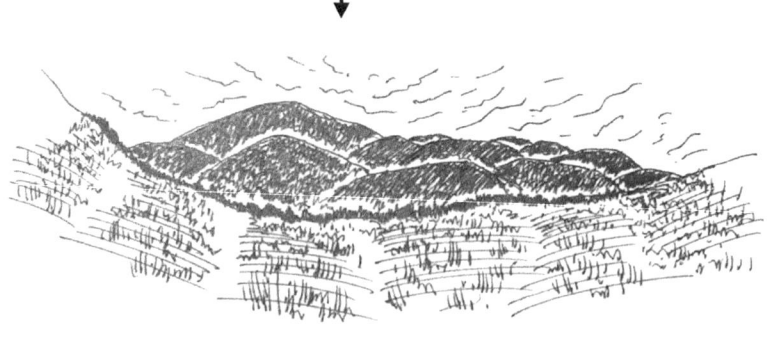

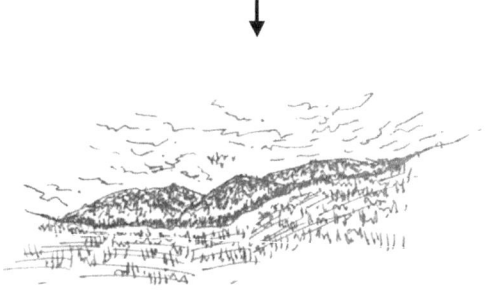

Drawing Hills with Slice:

Slice refers to a cut in the side making it flat as compared to overall rounded form without a slice. This often add more visual interest to a hill.

Slice

Draw a line like this to create a slice

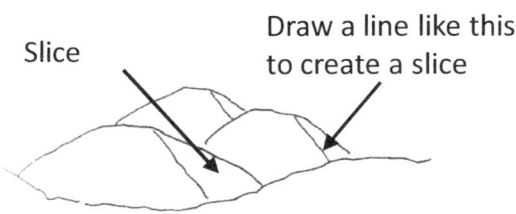

Some more examples

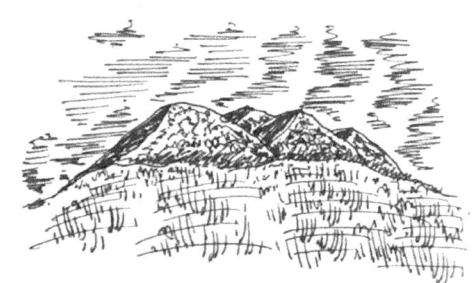

Slice should be darker than other side

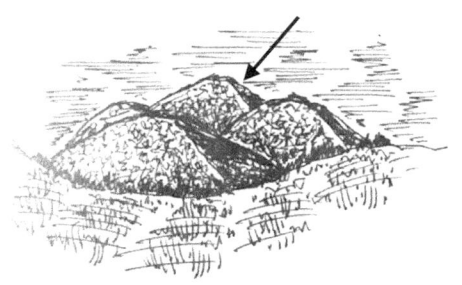

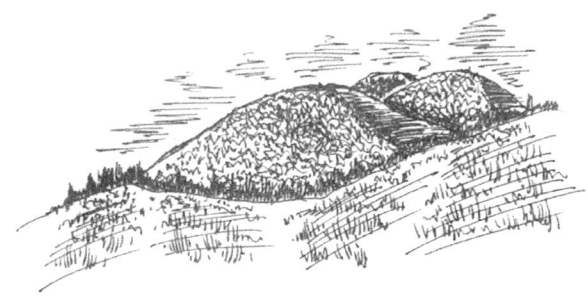

A Path Leading to Top of Hill:

A Path leading to the top of the hill also adds visual interest and makes our eyes travel from foreground to the top of the hill. Always make the path tapered from foreground to the end. A path can even span multiple hills.

Always add a
path tapered

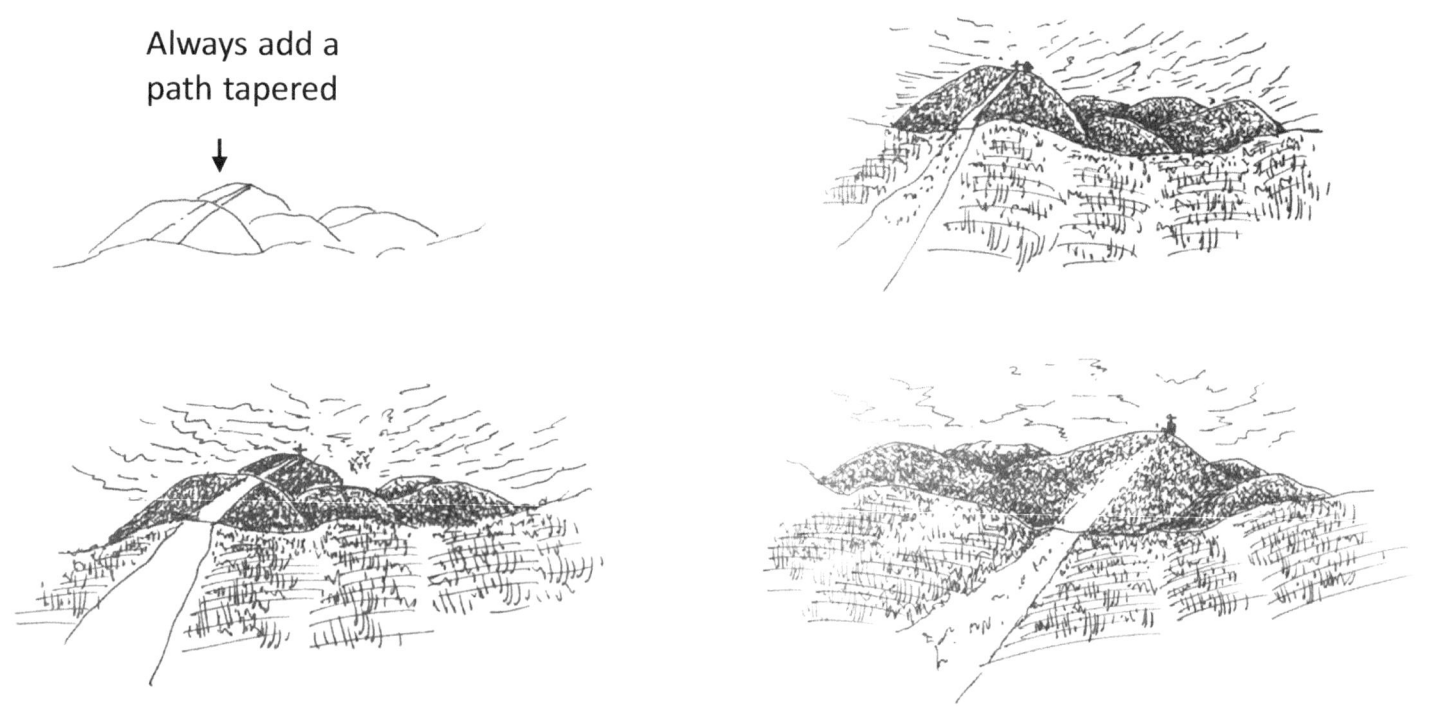

Trees on the Hill:

Another option is to also indicate trees on top of hills. This can be done by using small parallel lines or other techniques for indicating distant trees on top of hills. This adds a different feel to the hills.

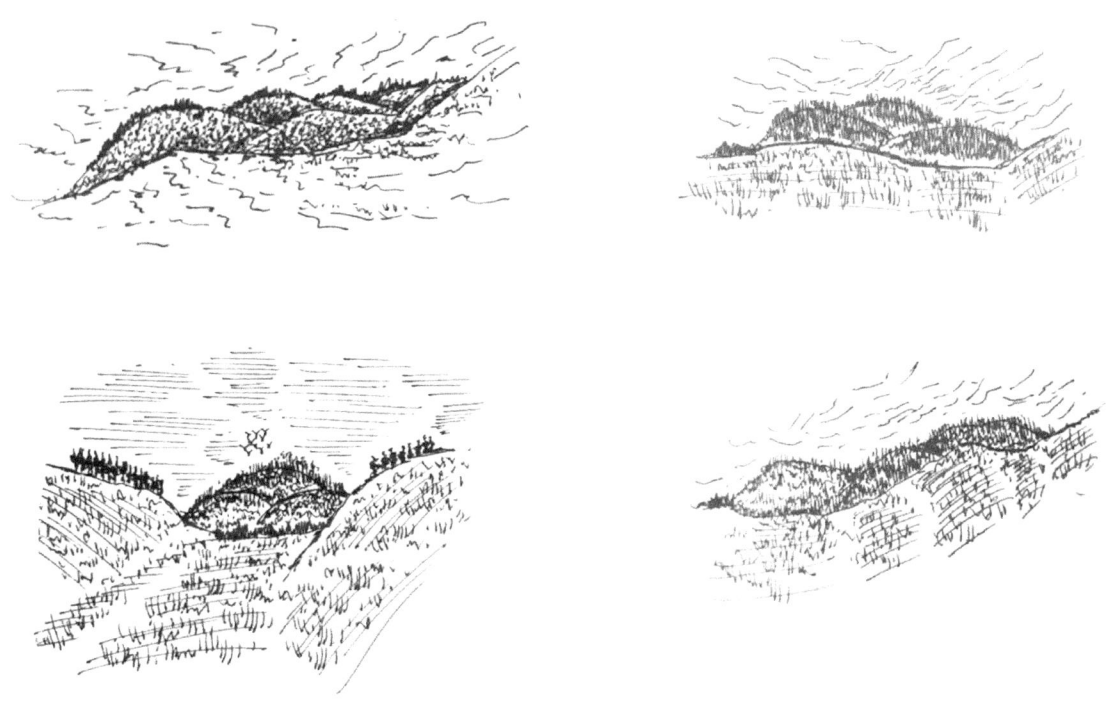

Drawing Distant Mountains:

Drawing mountains is covered extensively in vol. 4 of the series. You can find more information on other volumes at www.pendrawings.me/workbooks. Here we will focus on simple technique for texturing a distant mountain. A distant mountain in place or in addition to a distant hill provides a great background element for landscapes.

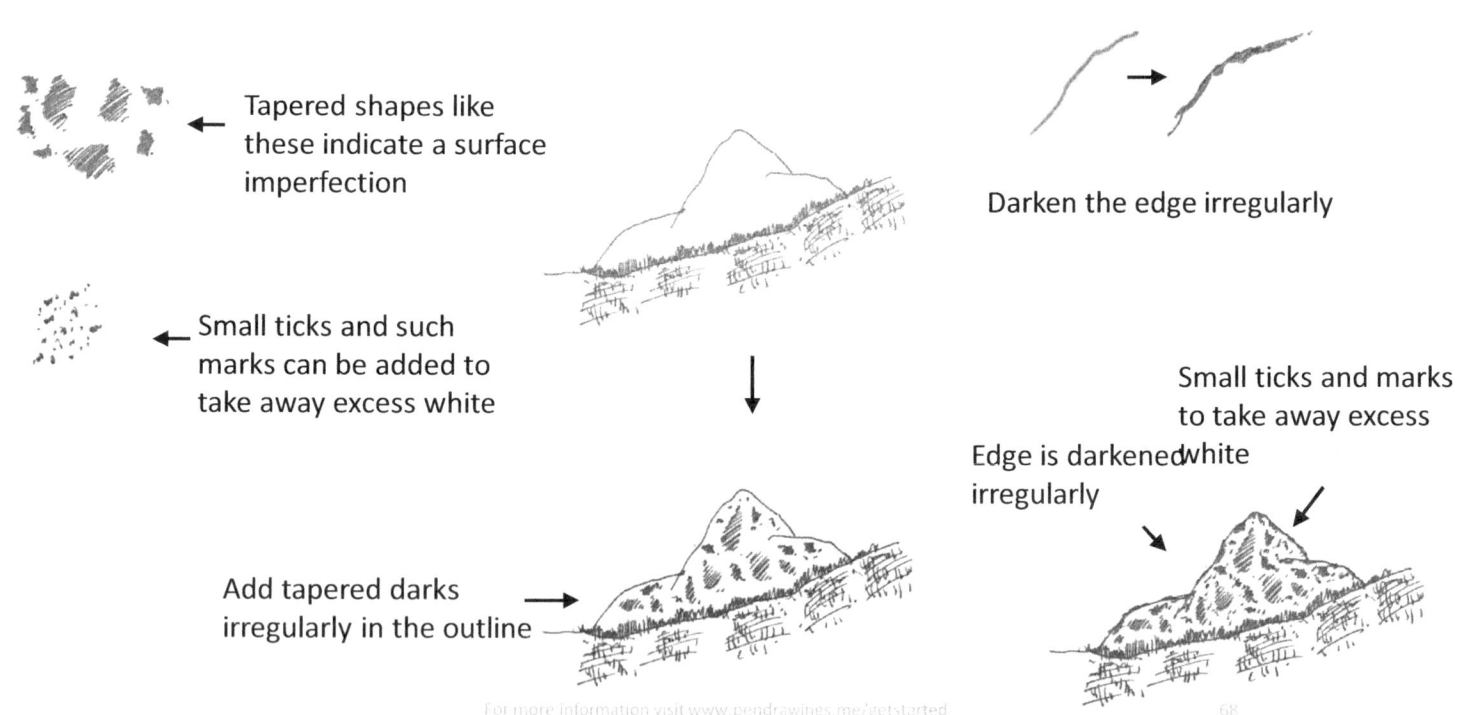

Tapered shapes like these indicate a surface imperfection

Small ticks and such marks can be added to take away excess white

Darken the edge irregularly

Add tapered darks irregularly in the outline

Edge is darkened irregularly

Small ticks and marks to take away excess white

Drawing Distant Mountains, More Examples:

Here are some more examples of using tapered dark to texture mountains. This is a very versatile technique and mountains in many different shapes and sizes can be textured using this technique.

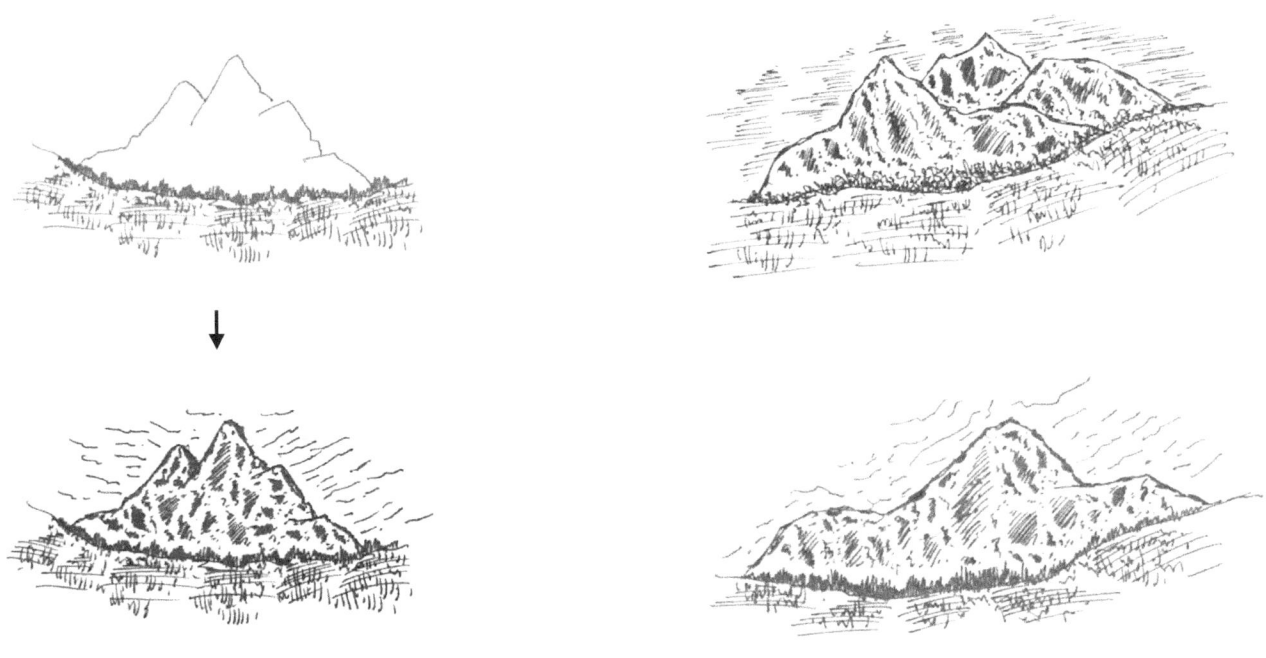

Drawing Distant Mountains, Another Technique:

Here is another technique for drawing background mountains using dots and ticks. Key here is to create interesting outline that brings out the feel of mountains in the drawing.

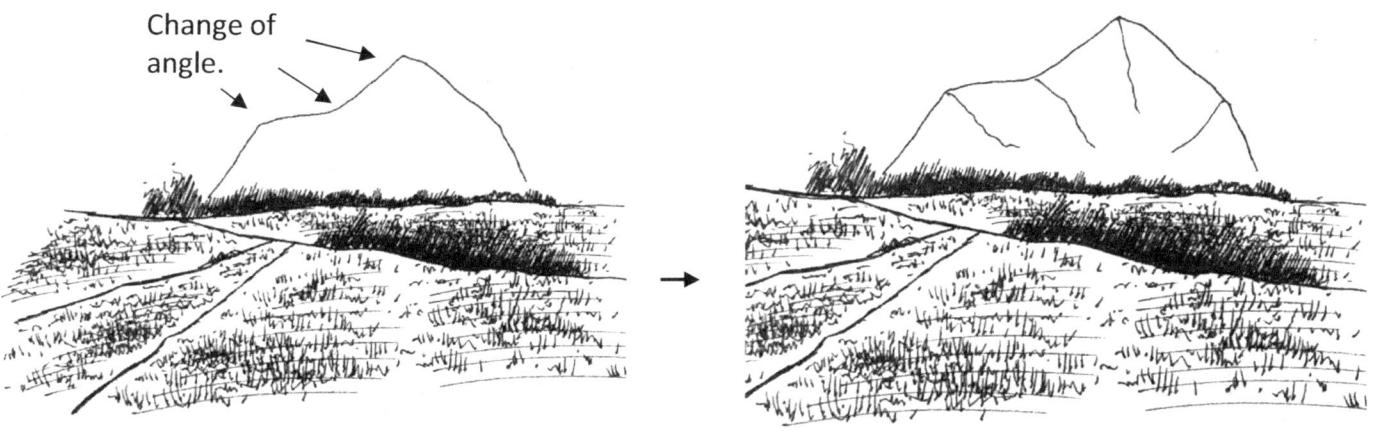

Draw an outline with change of angles as shown above.

From change of angle point, draw lines as shown above to create plains.

Drawing Distant Mountains, Another Technique, Continued:

This technique is discussed in detail in vol. 4 of workbook series. Please visit www.pendrawings.me/workbooks for more information.

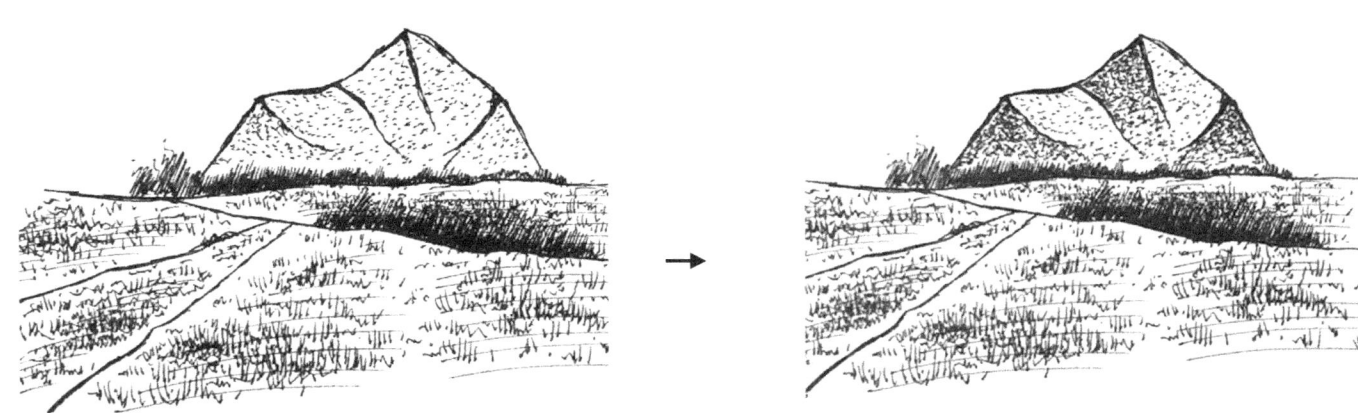

Use dots and ticks to initially texture the mountain.

Add more dots and ticks to make the vertically oriented plains darker.

Concept of Tonal Variation:

On a flat drawing surface, an object can appear 3 dimensional due to change in volume of tone (light and dark) employed on its surface. Those sides of an object facing the light source are lit brighter (less tone) than the sides away from the light source (indicated darker using more tone). For a mountain, we assume that Sun is primary light source and is assumed to be overhead. Under this assumption, vertical plains will receive less light and are textured darker than horizontal surfaces.

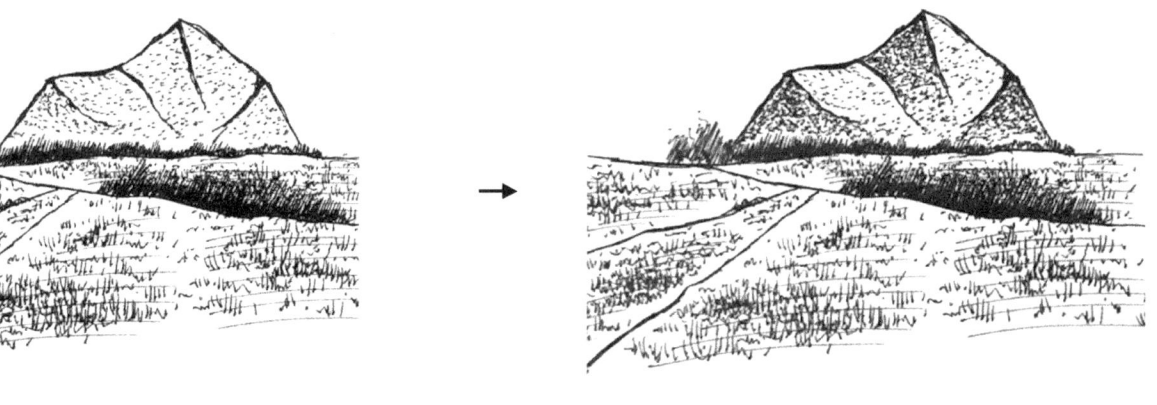

Use of single tone doesn't bring out the dimensionality of the mountain.

By using different tones as discussed above, the mountain acquires its form.

Another Example:

Following is another example. Notice again the use of angular outline to create plains in the body of mountain and use of different tones to bring out the plains. This is discussed in more detail in vol. 4 of my pen and ink drawing workbooks (**www.pendrawings.me/workbooks**).

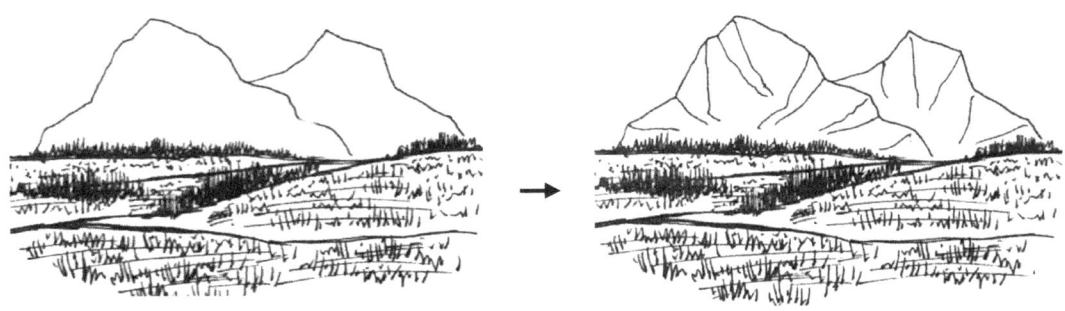

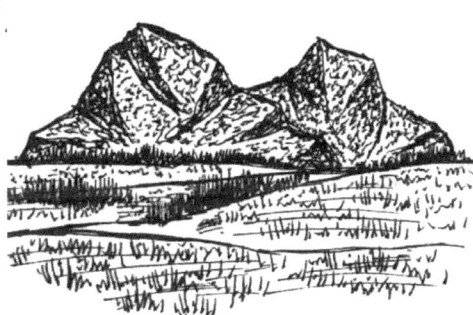

This is a very versatile technique. By using different shapes, mountains with very different feel can be drawn. Draw plains at different angles and spread them irregularly to give mountain more visual interest.

Activity: Drawing Distant Mountains:

Practice texturing mountains in the outlines below per earlier instructions. Draw some of your own.

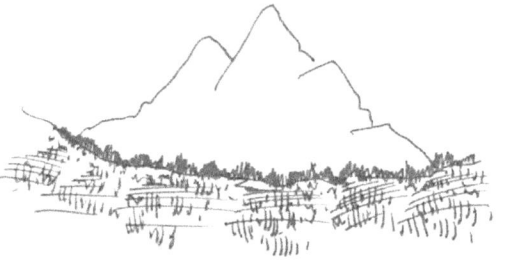 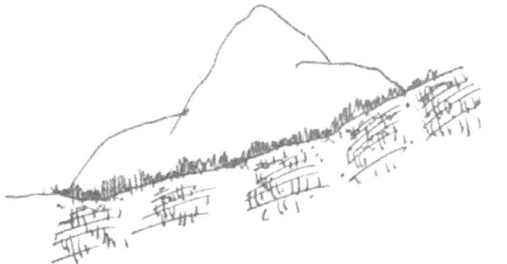

Drawing Mountains With Slice:

Tapered slices just like hills can be added to mountains as well as shown below. Always make the slice darker. Rest of texturing is same as before.

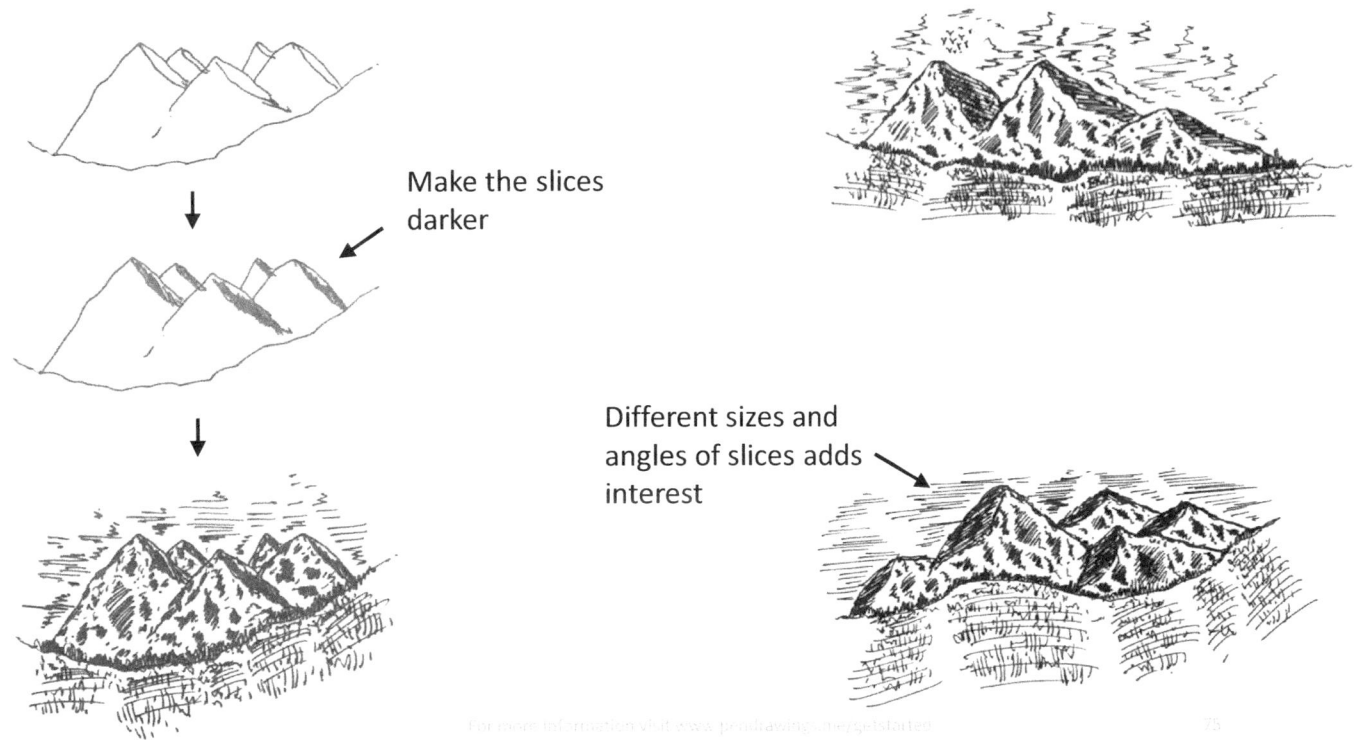

Make the slices darker

Different sizes and angles of slices adds interest

Drawing Mountains With Other Techniques:

In vol. 4 of the workbook series, I cover different techniques for drawing mountains. Those other techniques can be also used to create mountains with different feel. Pl. refer to that volume for more information. You can find more information on different volumes at www.pendrawings.me/workbooks.

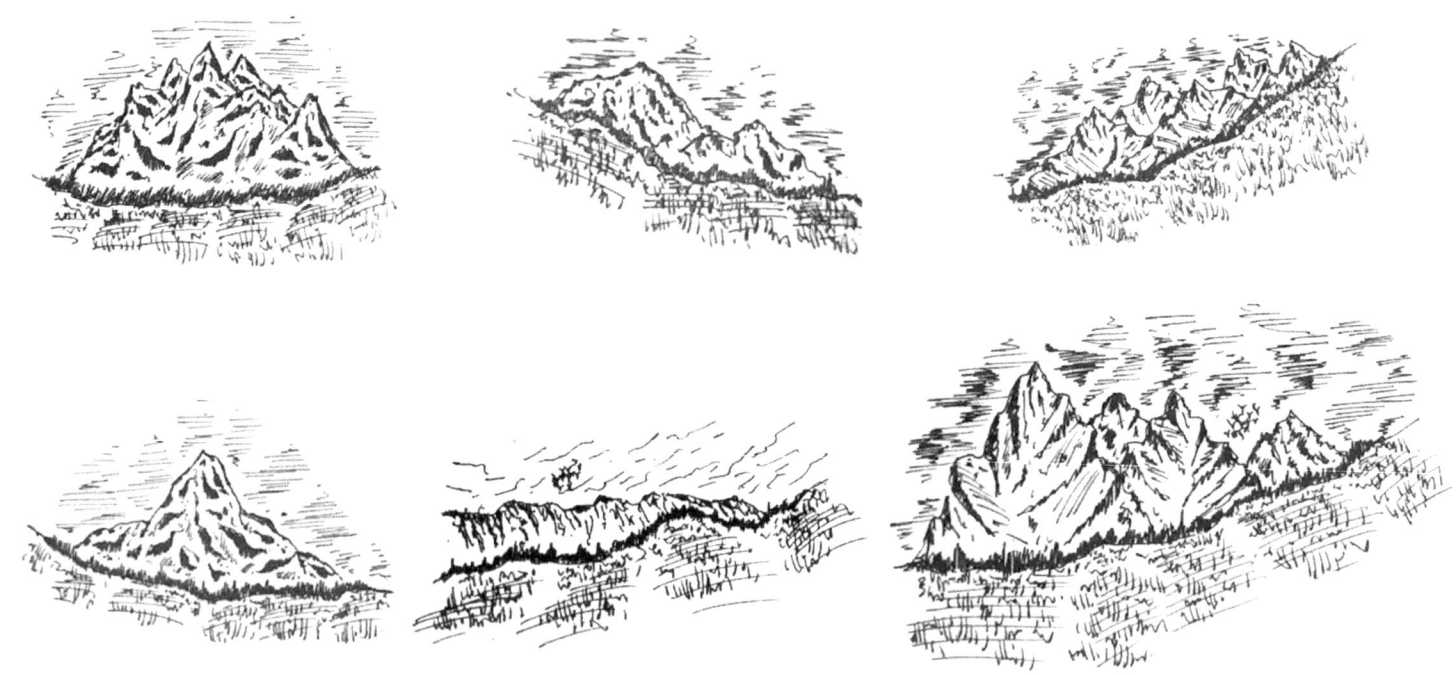

Combining Mountains and Hills:

Mountains and hills are both background elements and can be combined to add more visual interest to the drawing. Hills are in the front with mountains looming over them. Following are some examples. Techniques used are same as discussed earlier for drawing hills and mountains.

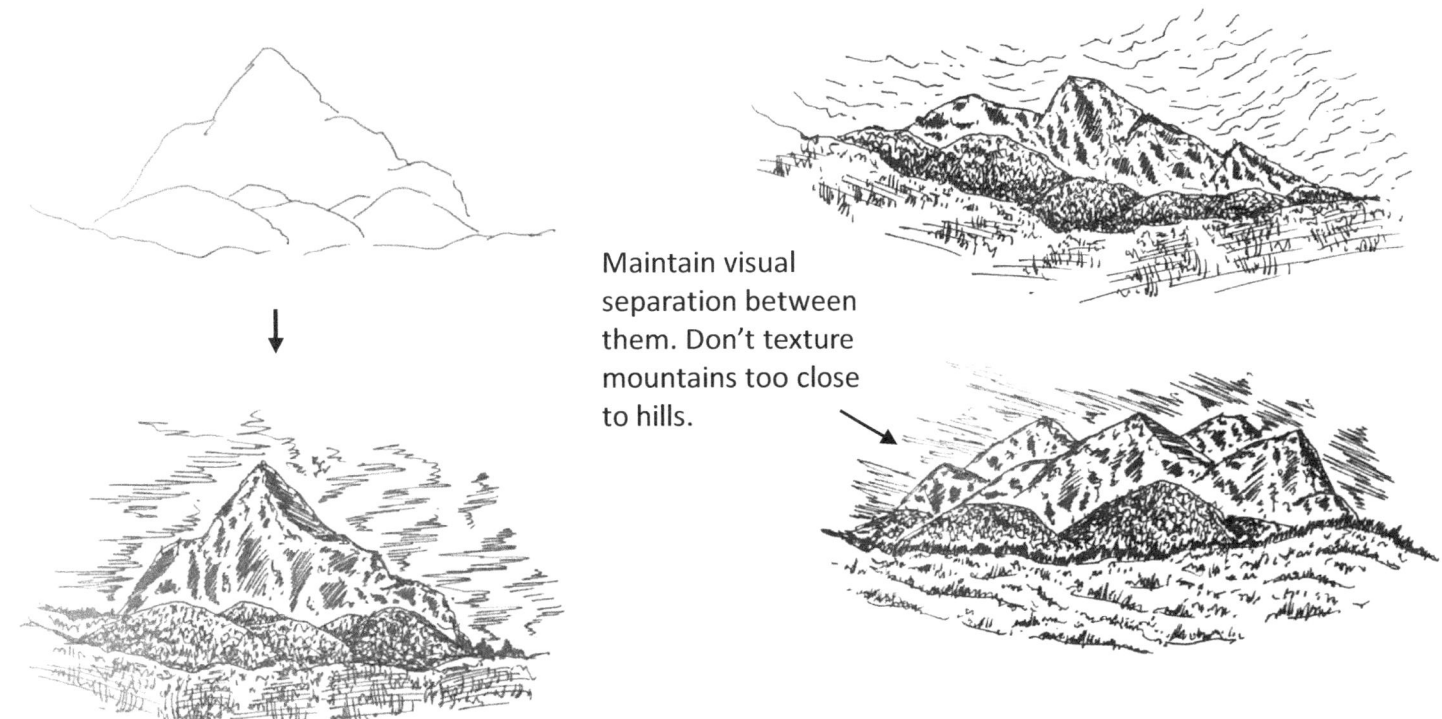

Maintain visual separation between them. Don't texture mountains too close to hills.

Activity: Combining Mountains and Hills:

Practice drawing mountains and hills combined per earlier instructions. Draw more of your own.

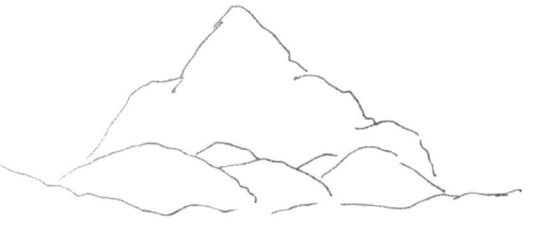

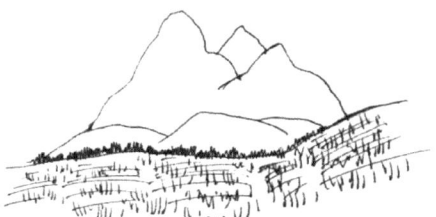

Drawing Snow Covered Mountains:

Snow covered mountains are visually very appealing and can be easily drawn as shown below.

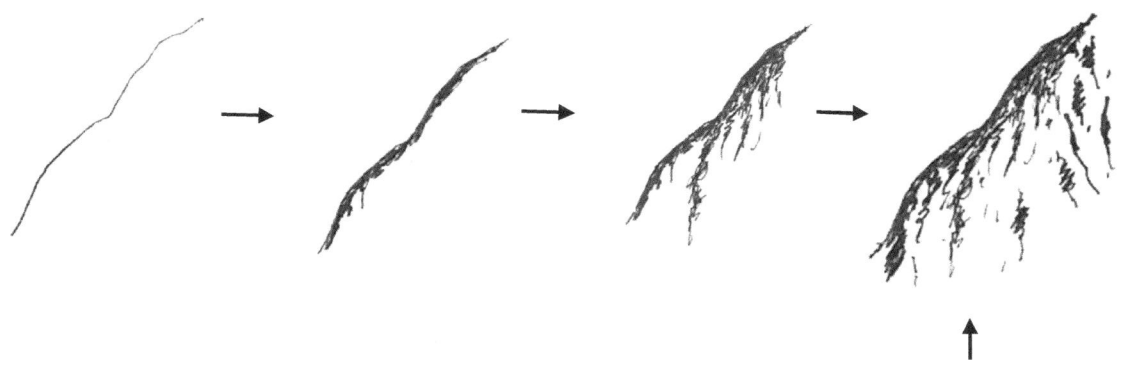

Key to depicting snow is to draw the edges in this manner by darkening it irregularly. By using the tapered darks shown, darken the edges as shown above to give feel of snow.

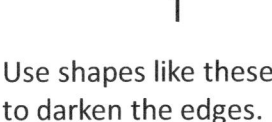

Use shapes like these to darken the edges.

Step by Step Drawing Snow Covered Mountains:

Darken the edges as shown in last page to bring out the feel of snow.

Snow rests usually in the main body of the mountain. Also snow creates irregularly darkened edges as shown. By bringing it out, feel of snow is depicted.

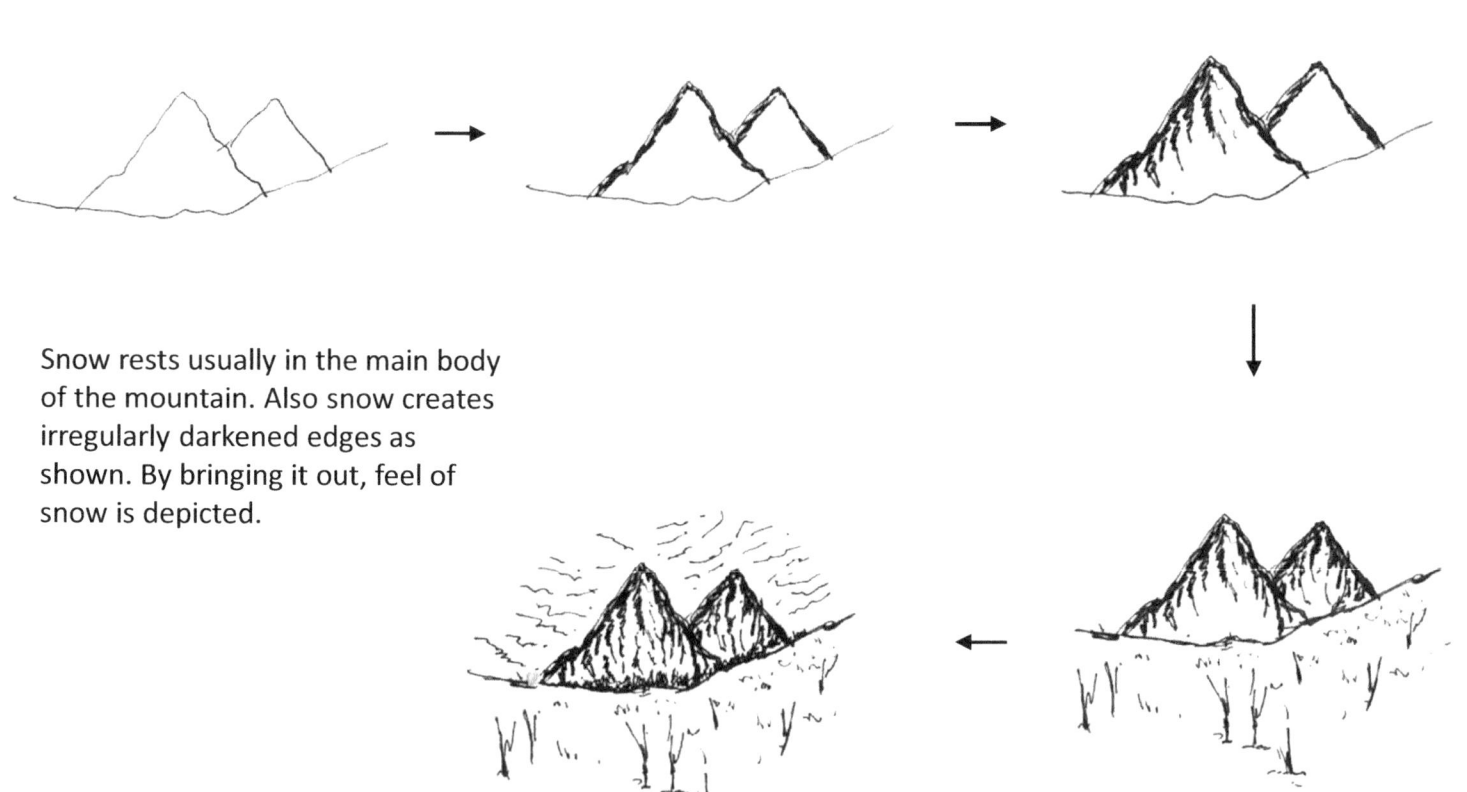

Some more examples of Snow Covered Mountains:

Below are some more examples of snow covered mountains drawn using the last technique.

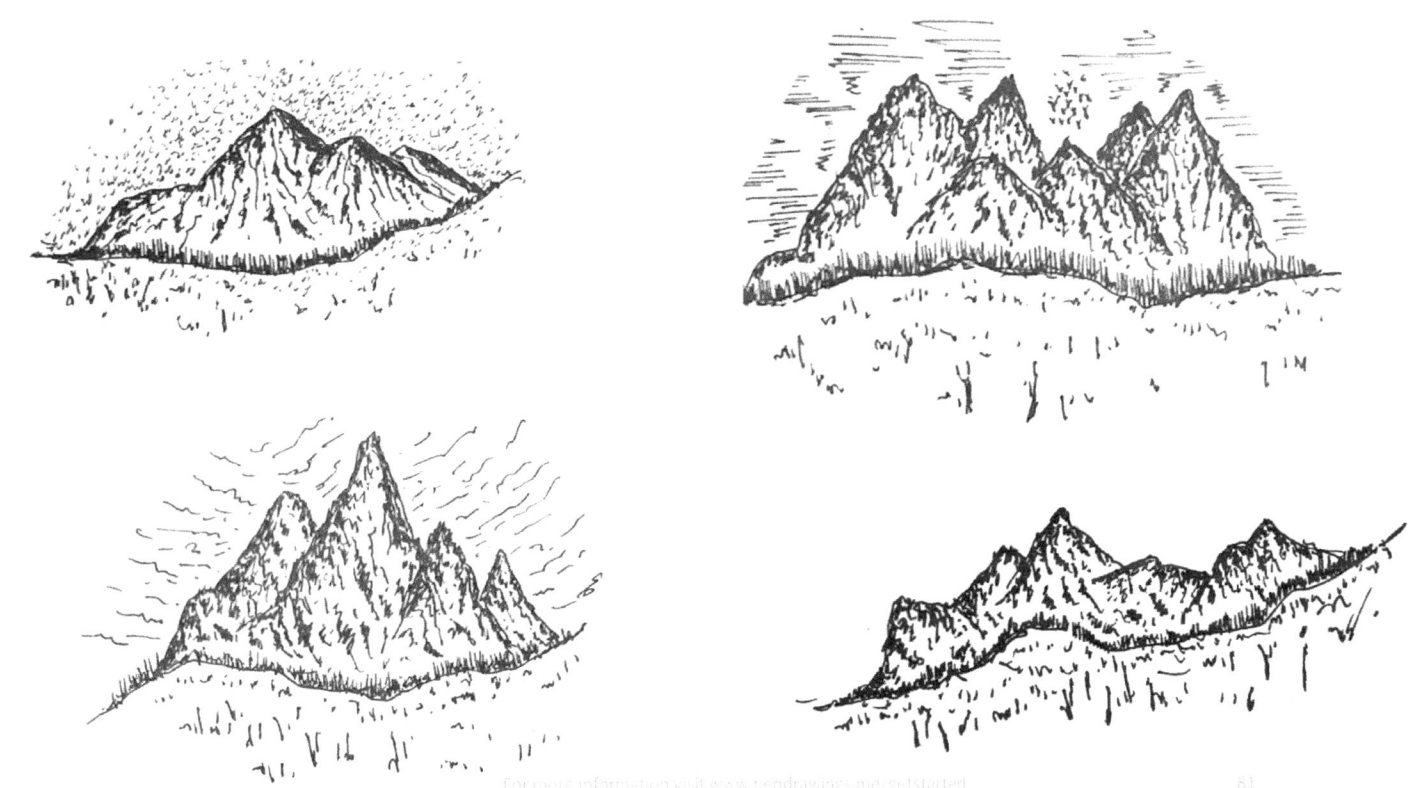

Activity: Drawing Snow Covered Mountains:

Practice darkening the edges below to give a feel of snow as discussed before. Also texture the mountain.

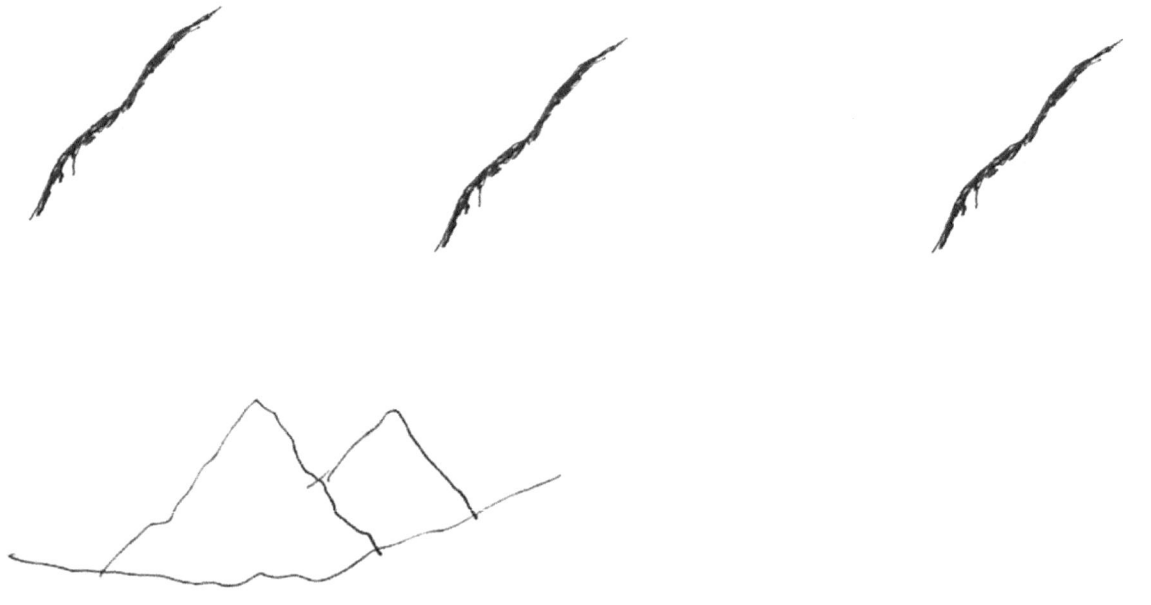

Texturing Ground for a Snow Covered Feel:

Snow covered ground goes well with a snow covered mountain. To give a feel of snow covered ground, just use few hinds of grass and add twigs and sticks poking out as show below. Such twigs poking out give the feel of ground covered with snow as indicated by the white of the paper.

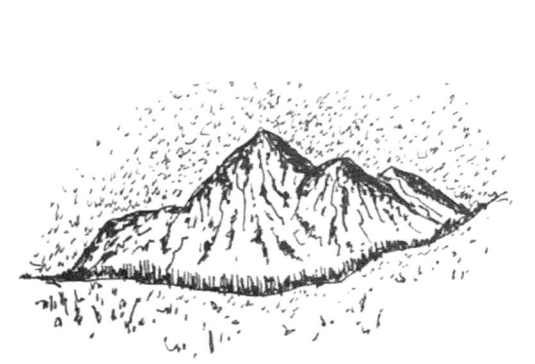
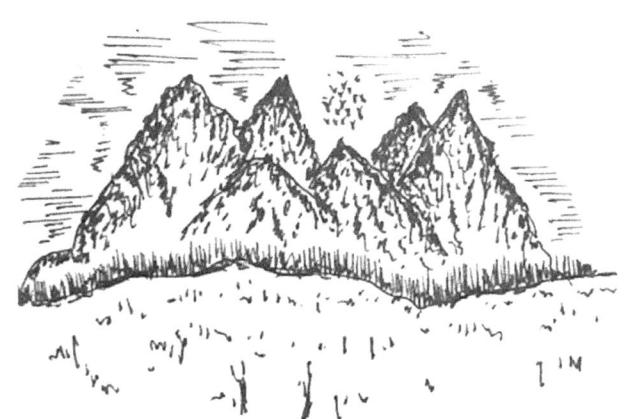

Another Technique for Drawing Snow Covered Mountains:

Following is another technique for drawing snow covered mountains. In this technique, the mountains is mostly textured dark using parallel lines with the white of snow left out to stand against the dark body.

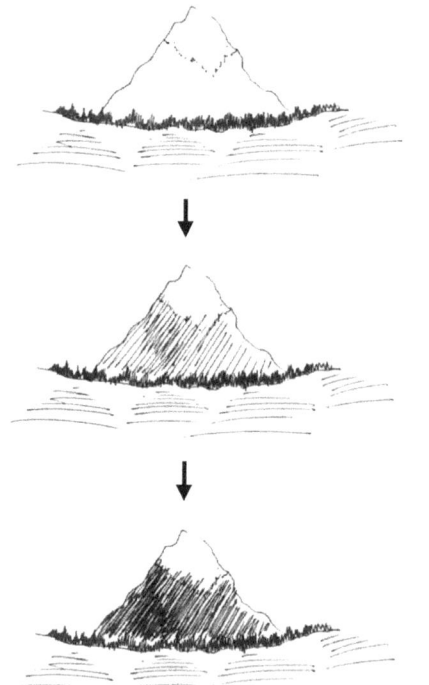

Draw the mountains outline and mark snow with dotted line.

Use parallel lines to texture the body leaving out the snow area.

Use additional sets of parallel lines to darken the body to contrast against the snow.

Another Technique for Drawing Snow Covered Mountains Continued:

This technique gives a feel of snow on mountains peaks where as the last technique gave a feel of mountains covered with snow. Use a lighter foreground and sky to contrast with the darker mountains in this technique.

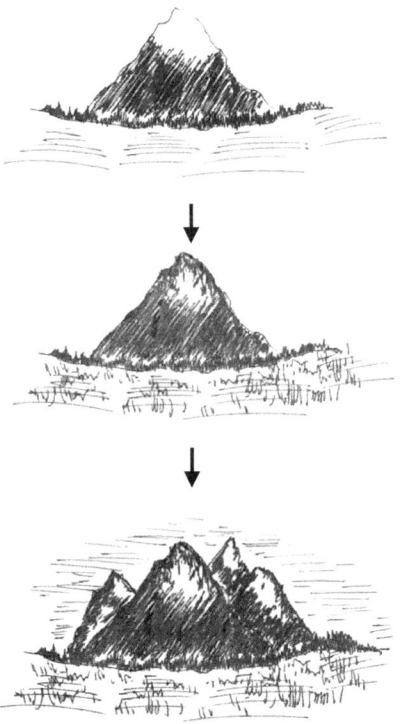

Darken the body with parallel lines. Keep the snow edge irregular.

Edges of the mountain can be darkened as well.

Add other mountains and texture them similarly to bring out the feel of snow sitting on the mountain tops.

Activity: Drawing Snow Covered Mountains:

Practice drawing snow covered mountains as discussed in last technique.

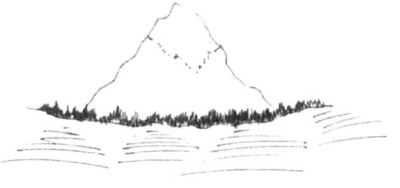

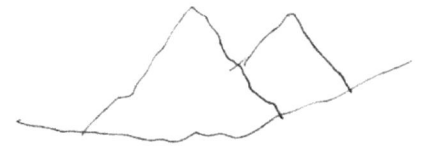

More Examples of Snow Covered Mountains:

Following are some more examples of technique discussed last. The high contrast in these drawings makes them eye catching and pleasing. Such mountains can be easily drawn from your imagination anytime.

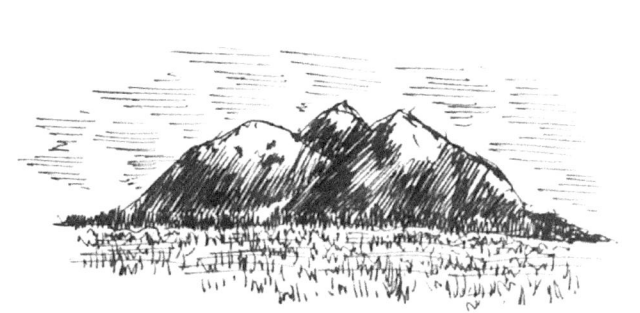
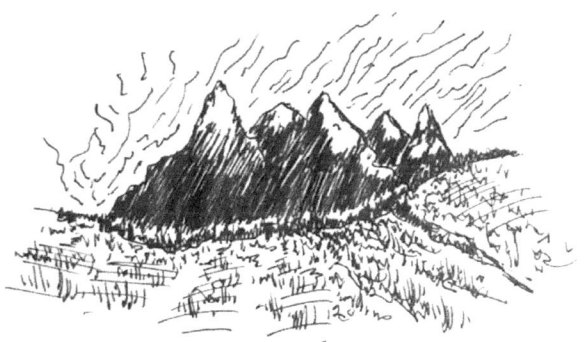

Step 6: Finishing with Sky:

As a final step, add Sky/Clouds to give it desired feel. Adding them is quite easy as we will see next and in addition to giving the drawing a finished feel, they can also be used to set the mood of the drawing.

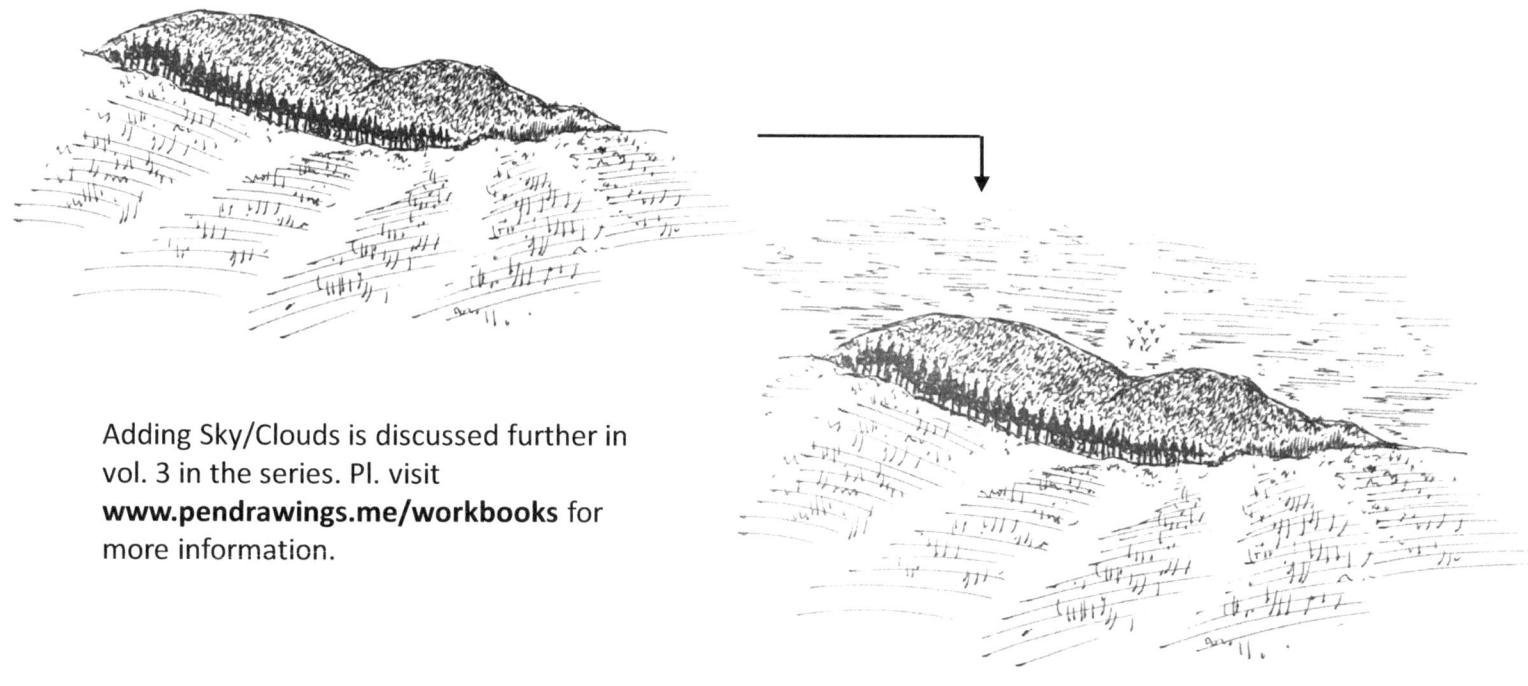

Adding Sky/Clouds is discussed further in vol. 3 in the series. Pl. visit **www.pendrawings.me/workbooks** for more information.

Adding Sky/Clouds:

Following is a very simple technique that can be used to give indication of Sky/Clouds and bring out the setting in the drawing.

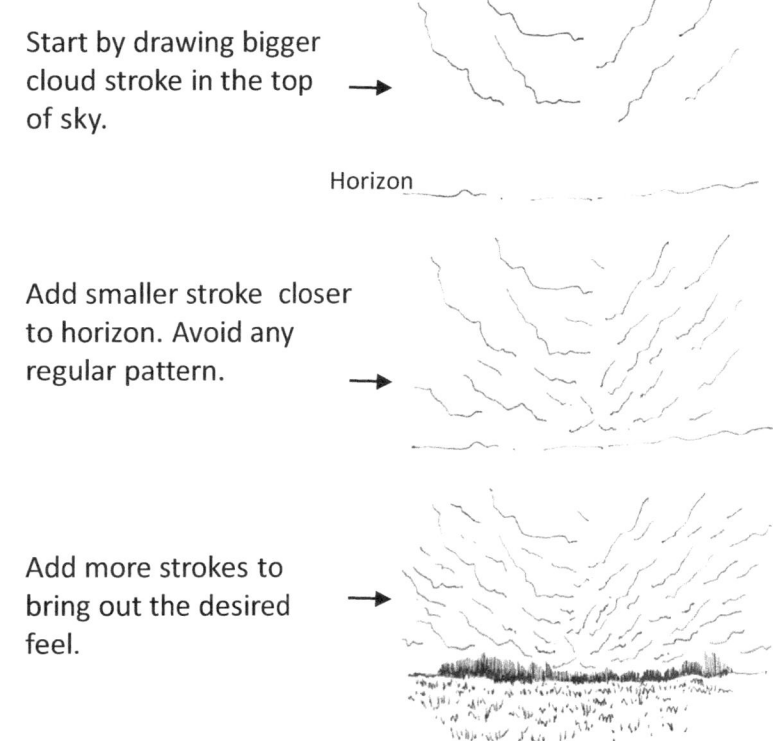

 ▲
Cloud Stroke used. These 'wandering' lines gives a feel of clouds

Start by drawing bigger cloud stroke in the top of sky. →

Add smaller stroke closer to horizon. Avoid any regular pattern. →

Add more strokes to bring out the desired feel. →

More Examples of the Technique:

Following are some more examples of using this technique. It is a very versatile technique and by changing, size, orientation and density of these lines, different feel for sky can be obtained.

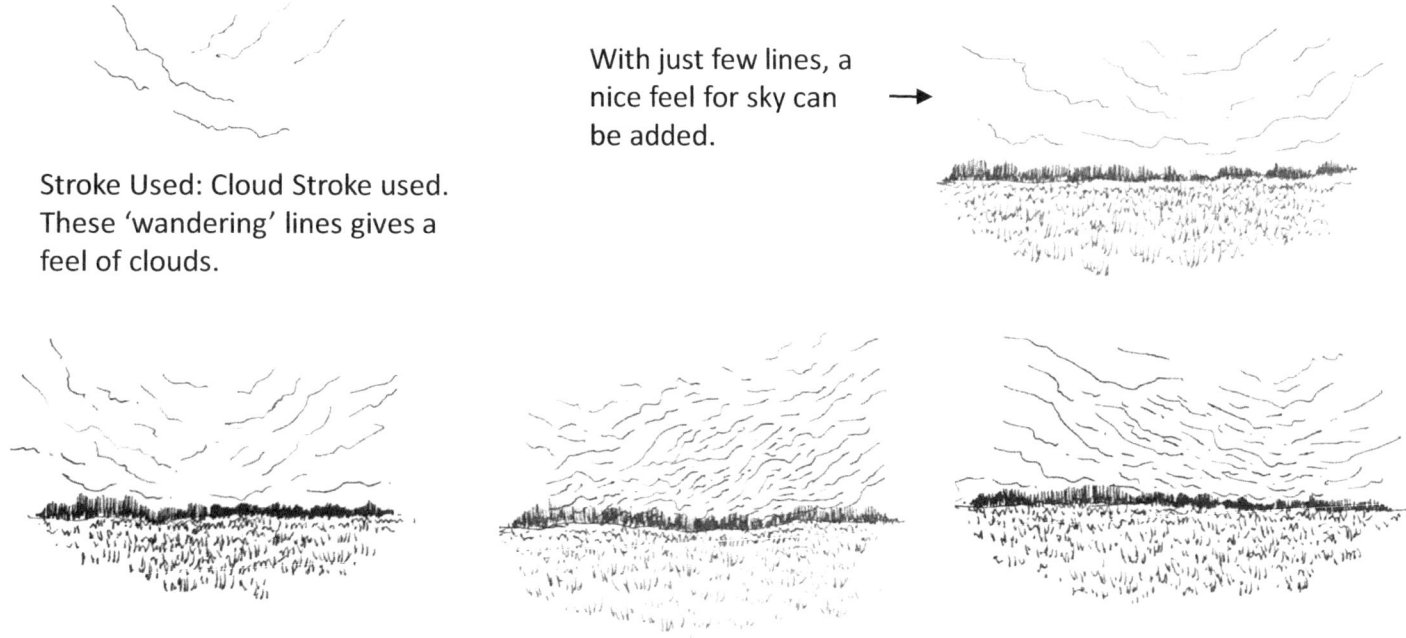

Stroke Used: Cloud Stroke used. These 'wandering' lines gives a feel of clouds.

With just few lines, a nice feel for sky can be added.

Another Technique for Drawing Sky/Clouds:

Following is another simple technique though it requires use of parallel lines. It can be used to indicate different kind of settings in your drawing.

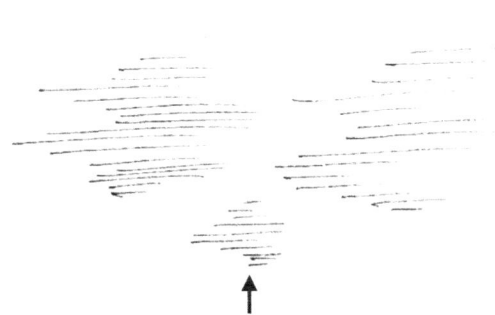

Stroke Used: Parallel lines in wavy manner

Smaller lines closer to horizon and bigger going up.

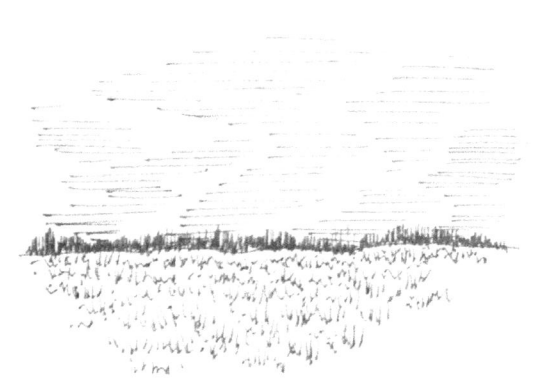

This is a very flexible technique. By changing nature of shape of parallel lines, different feel for sky can be obtained.

Study many examples of this technique in this book to understand its use.

Yet Another Technique for Drawing Sky/Clouds:

One of the simplest techniques for indicating Sky/Clouds is the use of dots and small ticks. By changing the density of these in different ways different feel for Sky can be obtained.

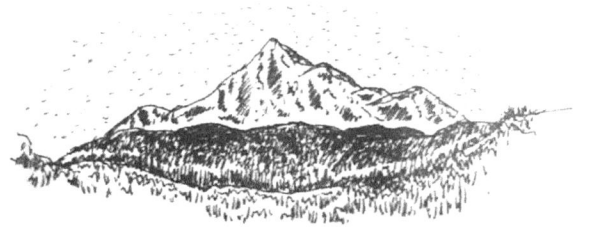

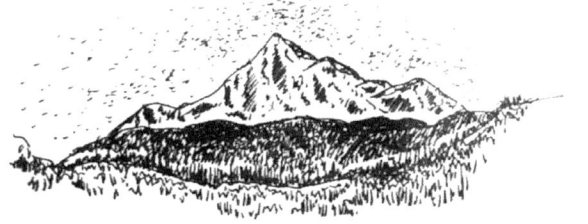

Low uniform density of dots. A generic non inviting backdrop.

Varied density with more near the top establishes a focal point there and makes our eyes travel to the top.

Yet more density with nice variations creates a very pleasing back drop for the mountains. ➡

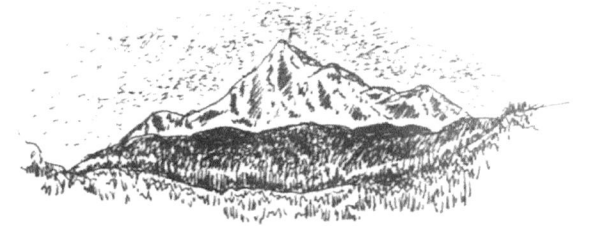

Activity: Drawing Sky/Clouds:

Add Sky/Clouds to the following drawings per earlier instructions. Also add them to drawings completed in earlier activities.

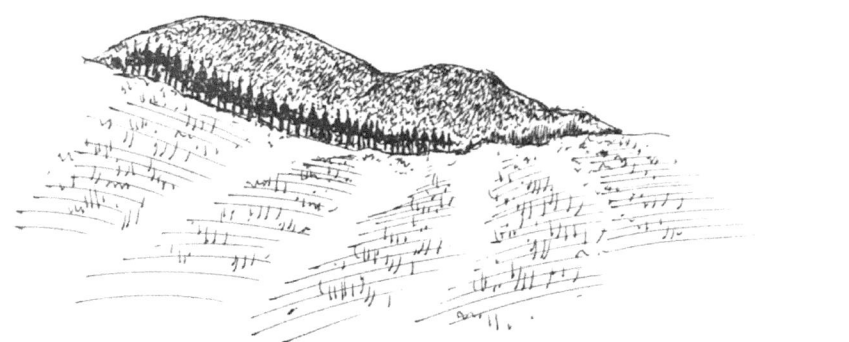
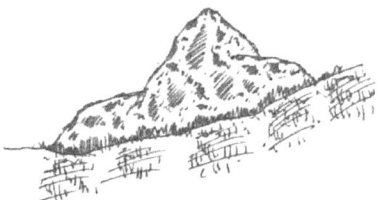

Adding Other Elements:

So far we have looked at how to draw plains from foreground to distant horizon, add ground contour and ground cover, indicate distant element and a backdrop of hills, mountains and Sky. Another consideration is addition of other elements on plains. This adds visual interest to the drawing.

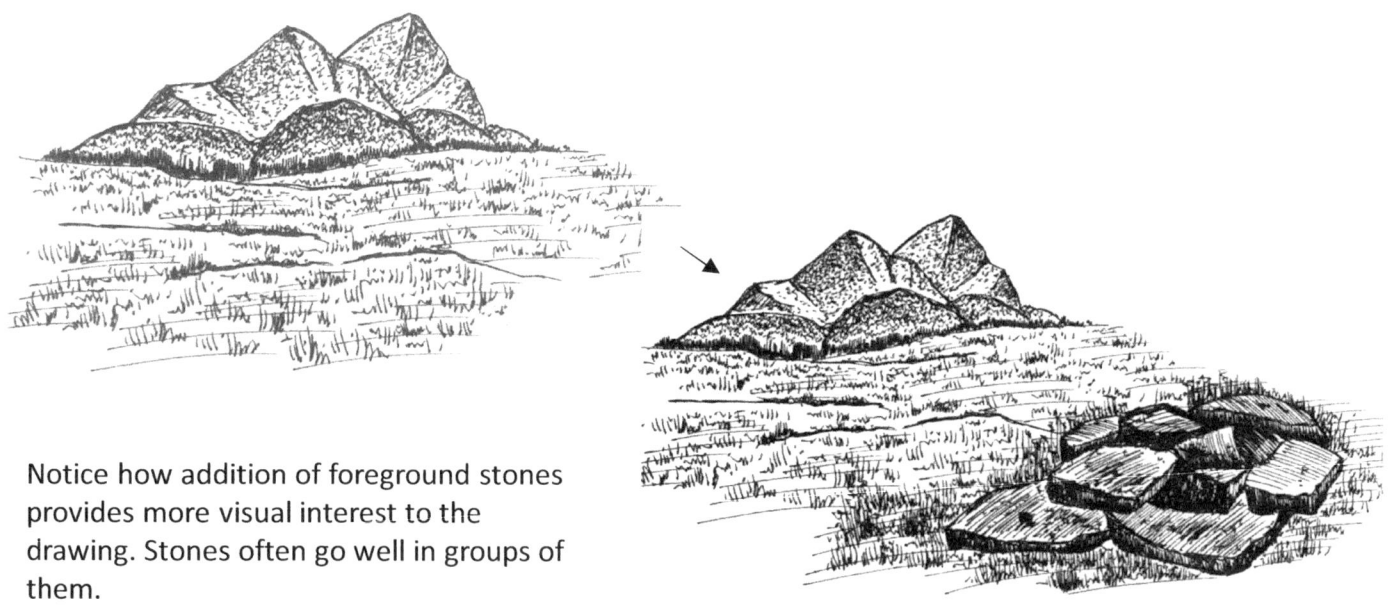

Notice how addition of foreground stones provides more visual interest to the drawing. Stones often go well in groups of them.

Order of Drawing Elements:

As there is no erasure in pen and ink drawing, it is always helpful to lay down elements on plains first. This way you don't have to worry about leaving appropriate space for them.

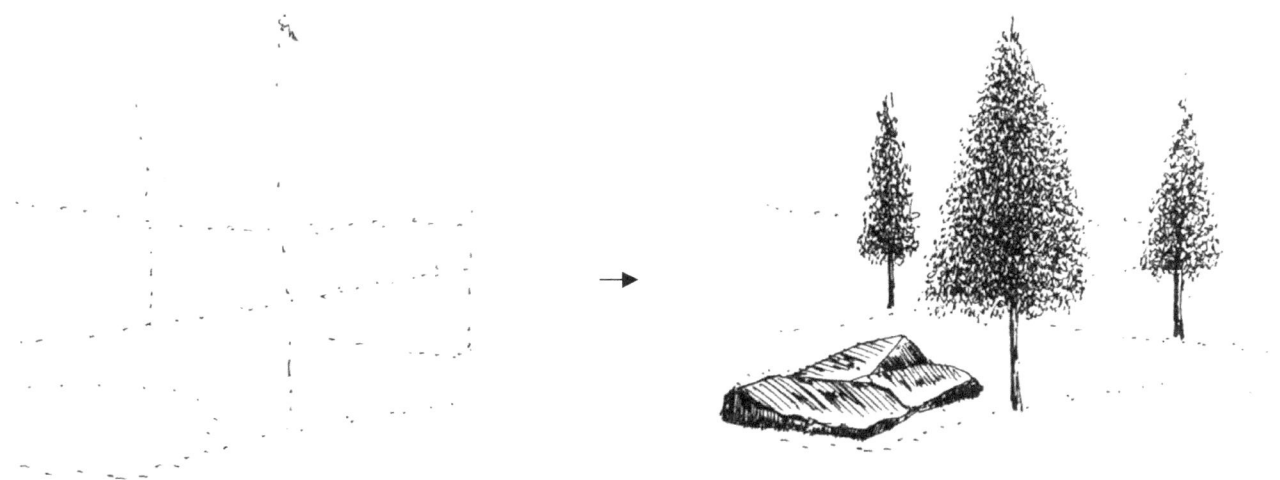

Don't put down hard plain lines in the beginning if you have elements over them. Here I have used dots to lay my initial plain lines and pine trees.

Elements on plains are initially drawn. Notice that plain lines should not be visible inside them. Using light dots for them ensures that.

Order of Drawing Elements, Continued:

By drawing elements in front first, you can also clearly see the space that is left for elements behind and work accordingly. As you gain more experience, you will be able to work interactively with different elements, but in the beginning, it is useful to go from front to back.

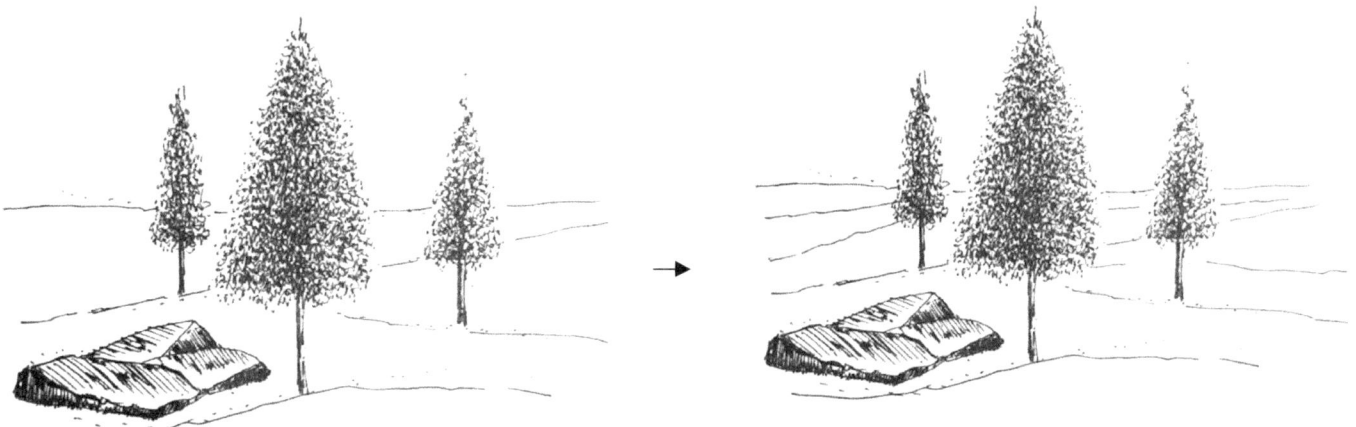

Plain lines should be fully drawn only after all elements crossing them are drawn.

Don't be afraid to improvise. Here I have added few more far away plains to take away excess white and add more visual interest.

Order of Drawing Elements, Continued:

After plain lines are put down, surface contours, ground cover and background can be drawn.

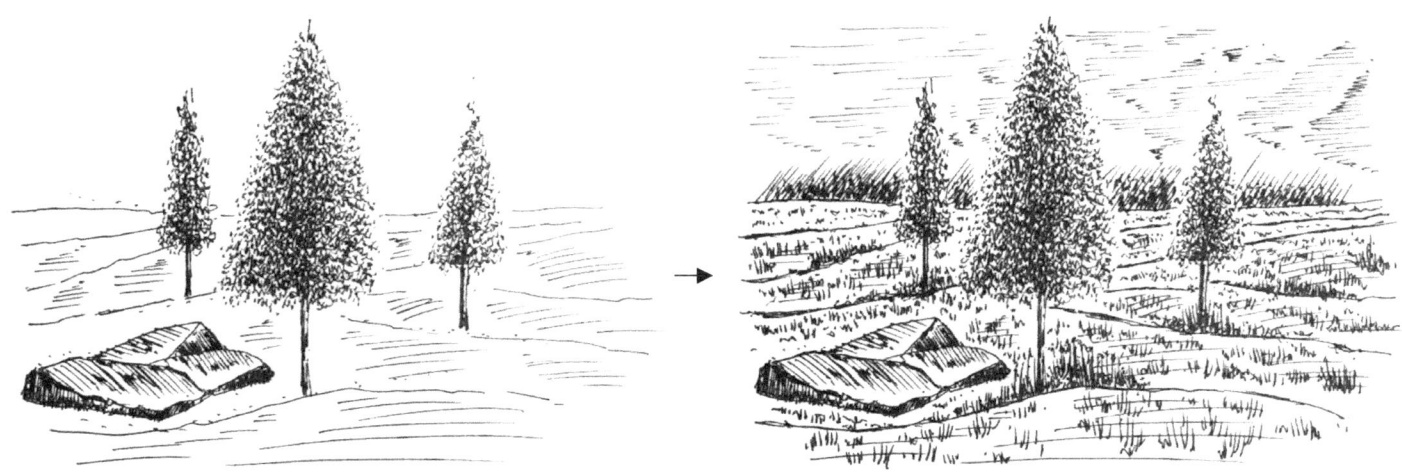

By drawing the pine trees in the beginning, we can see the space left for distant tree line and draw it appropriately. It is much easier than leaving space and trying to fit foreground and other elements in it later.

Let Your Imagination Flow:

Instead of focusing on plains initially, you can focus on the type and distribution of different elements in the beginning. Plain lines can next be added based on the layout of the elements as shown below.

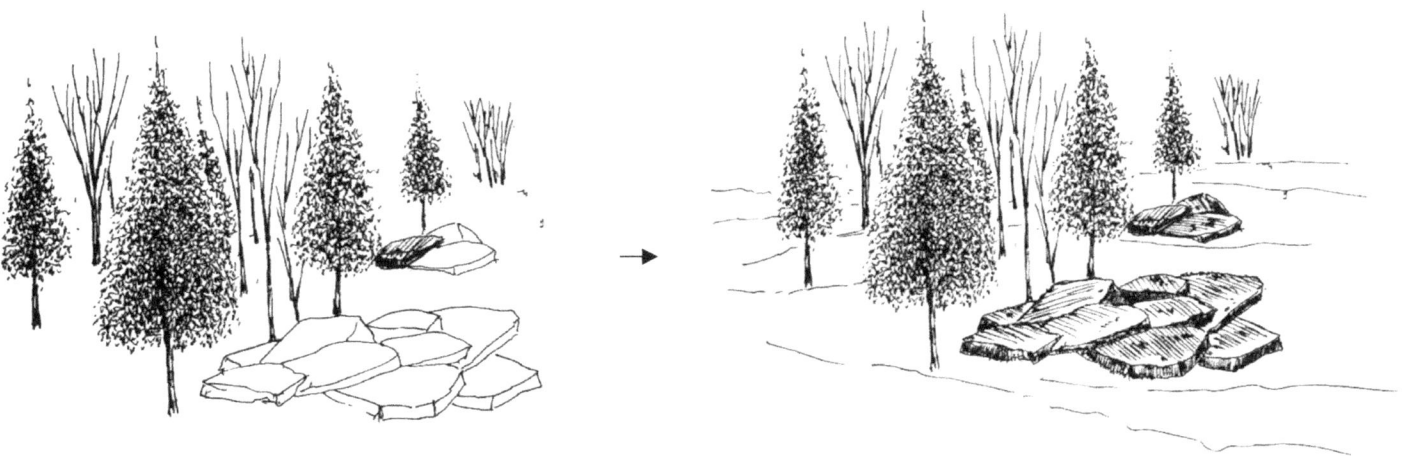

I start by laying down pine trees, bare winter trees and stones initially. Per perspective, elements farther out are drawn smaller. Here I don't start with plains in mind but instead fit them to the elements of my liking. Let your imagination flow and interactively add elements and plains to bring out the feel you like.

Let Your Imagination Flow, Continued:

The steps and order of adding elements we have looked at so far is an aid to help you make sense of drawing an involved landscape. But don't let it stop you from interactively improvising your drawings as you become more comfortable with the process.

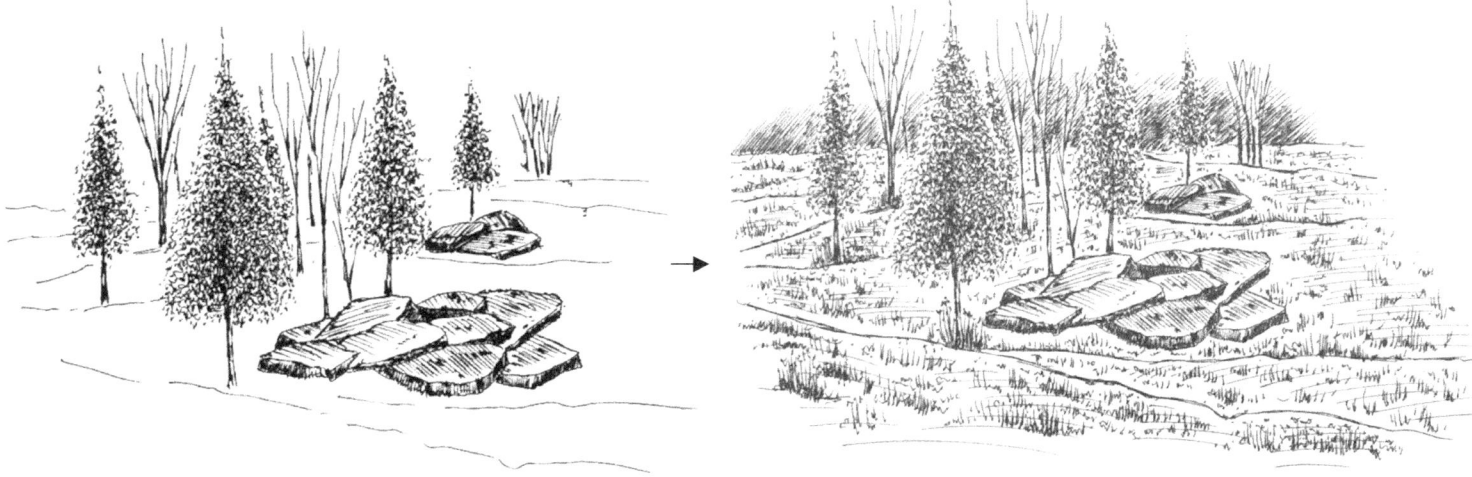

On the same set of elements, different plain lines can be used quite differently to bring out a different feel. Don't be afraid to experiment. Carry a pocket sketch book with you and play with drawing different combination of plains and elements to see the feel they evoke.

Drawing Pine Trees:

Next we look at how to draw different elements of nature. Here we will look at how to draw them at a small size with less details. Drawing them with more details at bigger size is discussed in other workbooks in the series. Pl. visit www.pendrawings.me/workbooks for more information.

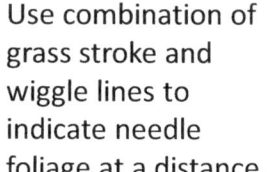

Use combination of grass stroke and wiggle lines to indicate needle foliage at a distance.

Use dots and ticks to create open edges.

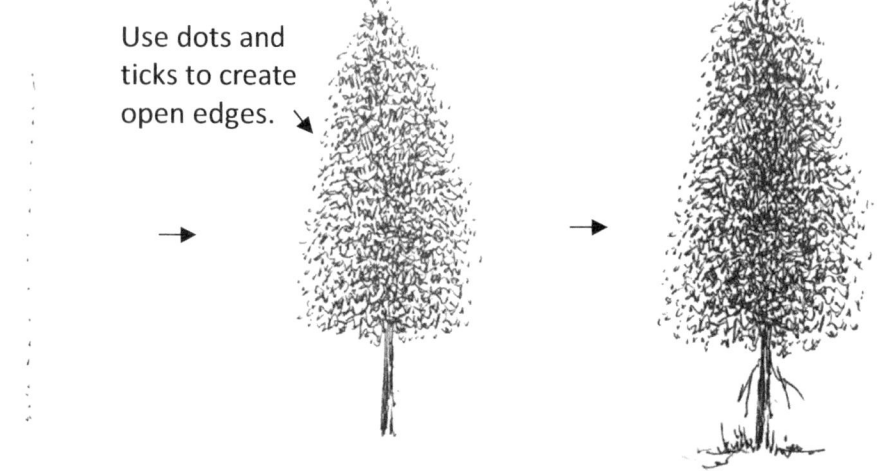

Start by laying down line indicating outline of the tree. Use the stroke indicated to initially texture and bring out the feel of needle foliage. Darken the center more to create tonal variation between the center and edges to bring out the depth.

Activity: Drawing Pine Trees:

Draw Pine Trees in the following outlines. Try some of your own.

Drawing Bare Winter Trees:

Bare winter trees are very easy to draw as solid tapered dark. Make sure there is evident taper in trunk and branches. Also use interesting shapes to add visual interest.

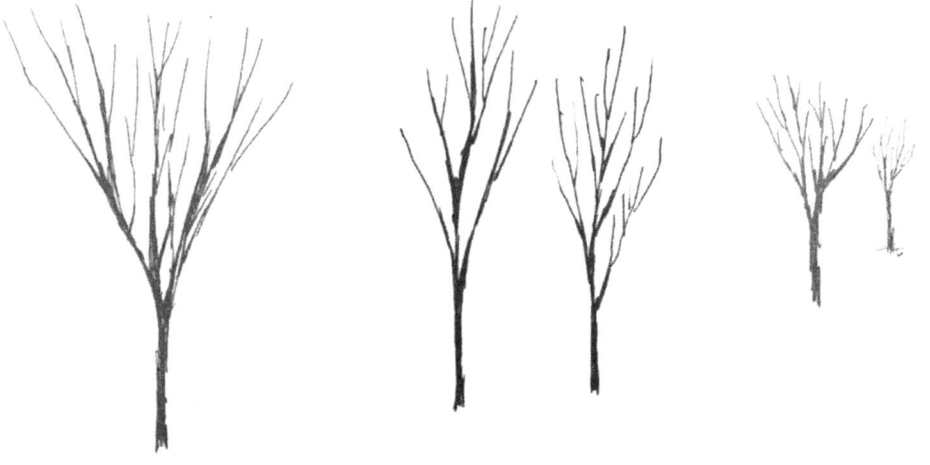

At a distance, bare winter trees can be easily drawn using solid tapered lines. Per perspective, make the ones closer to viewer bigger in size and progressively make them smaller as they go out in the distance.

Activity: Drawing Bare Winter Trees

Draw bare winter trees in the space below. Try different sizes, branch layout etc.

Landscapes with Pine and Bare Winter Trees:

Pine trees and bare winter trees can be used together to create very pleasing quick and easy winter landscapes. By using different volume and distribution of these, there is no limit to drawing landscapes based on them from your imagination. We have looked at some of these before. Following is another example.

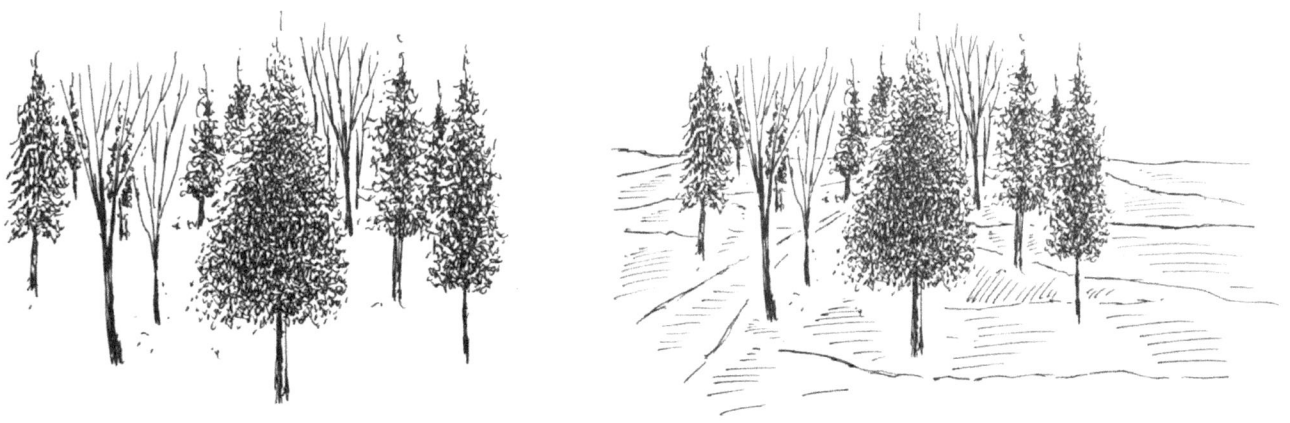

I start by laying down pine trees and bare winter trees to my liking. As pine trees have darker tone, distributing them between different sides creates a nice tonal balance. Bare winter trees can be added in between. Don't make the composition symmetrical as it looks unnatural. Next plain lines are added and contour lines added for ground form.

Landscapes with Pine and Bare Winter Trees, Continued:

Infinite variations are possible on this simple composition theme and one can be done from imagination anytime. Play with different volume, sizes, distribution, layout etc. for interplay between pine and bare winter trees. Different backdrop can be added to further add appeal to the drawing.

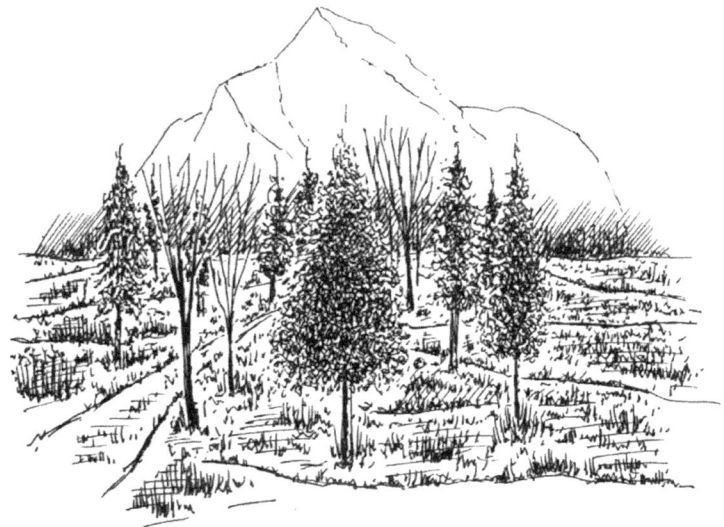

As the overall tone of the trees and ground is darker, I decided to leave just the outline of looming mountain which provides a nice contrast with the rest of the drawing. Experiment with such improvisations. Practice often and you will start to get feel for doing your own compositions.

Same techniques can be used to draw at a bigger scale in which case more details can be incorporated. Here is one of my drawings with pine trees and bare winter trees drawn at the size as printed.

Drawing a River:

Next we look at how to draw a river. River, or a flowing body of water can also be incorporated in many compositions effectively. Drawing water is covered extensively in detail in vol 4. of my workbook series. Pl. visit **www.pendrawings.me/workbooks** for more information.

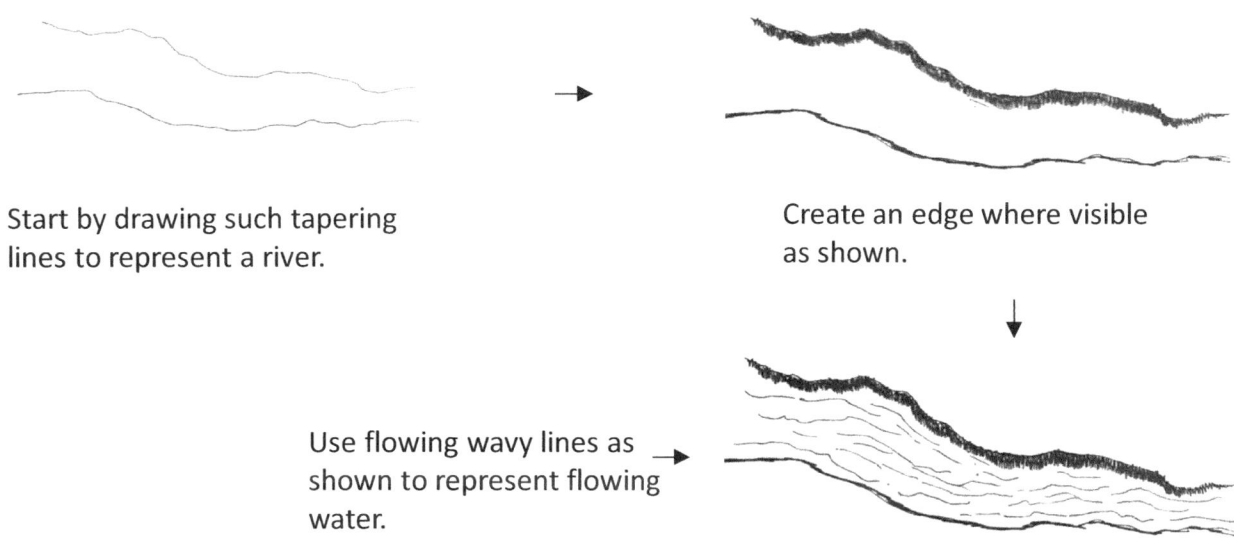

Start by drawing such tapering lines to represent a river.

Create an edge where visible as shown.

Use flowing wavy lines as shown to represent flowing water.

Drawing River, Continued:

Reflection of an object in it is important for our mind to interpret it as water. To add reflections, use more lines to increase tone in an irregular manner as shown below. Water is covered in detail in vol. 4 of the workbook series.

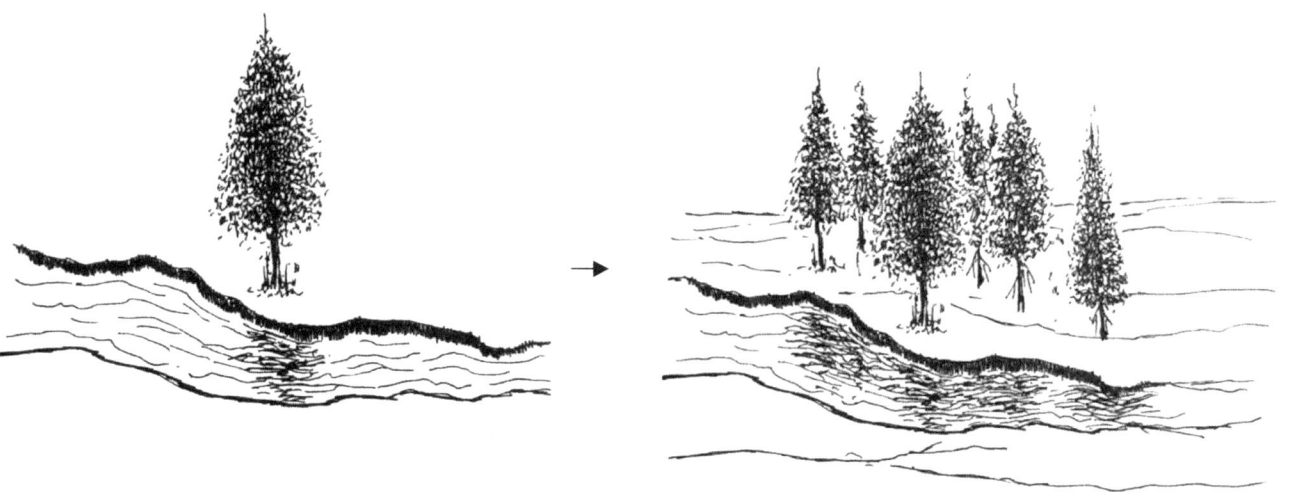

In a flowing water, reflection is hazy. Use more water lines to create darker hazy tone to indicate reflection as shown above. Add appropriate reflections for all elements near the river as shown.

Activity: Drawing River:

Draw river in the following outline. Also draw pine tress with their reflection in the water.

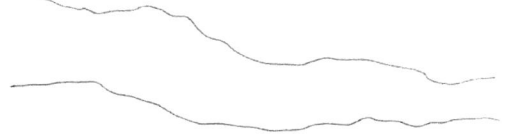
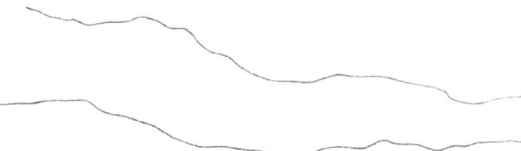

Landscapes with River:

Below is a quick landscape incorporating a river with pine trees reflected in it. Earlier landscapes we saw with pine trees and bare winter trees can be easily extended by incorporating a river closer to foreground.

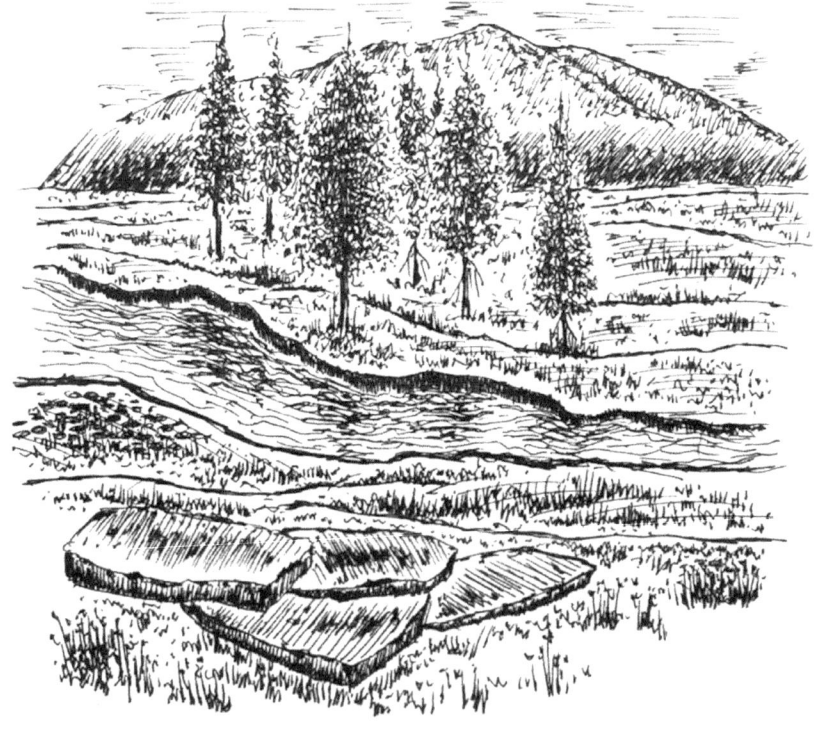

Keep the outline of river irregular and taper it slightly. Add some trees closer to river so that they will be reflected in the water. Elements far away from river will not reflect in water.

Landscapes with River, Another Example:

Following is another composition theme with a river. Limitless variations on this can be drawn from your imagination. Try one now.

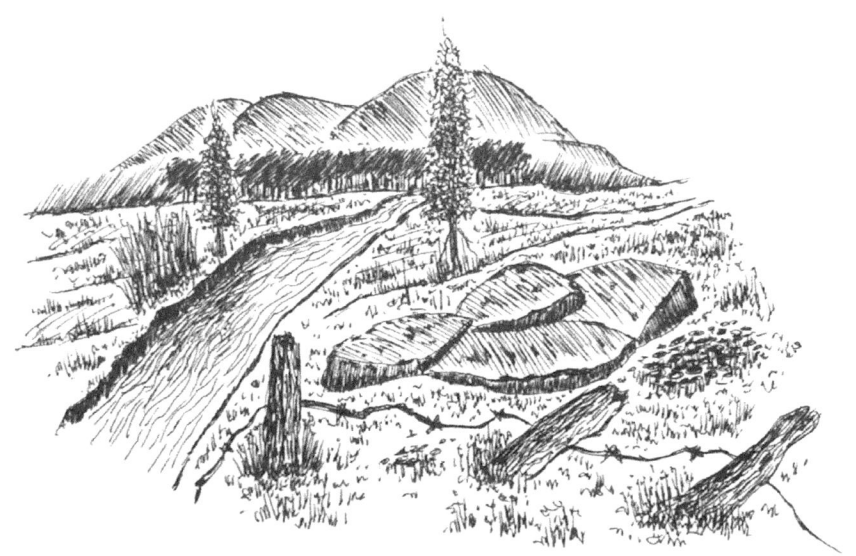

A River flowing from viewer to distant horizon is another common composition theme. Here I have used wooden posts in the foreground to add interest. They are discussed in detail later.

Drawing Stones:

Stones are the most common elements to be used in the foreground as we have seen in many landscapes already. We will look at a very simple way to draw them here. Drawing them is covered in detail in vol. 3 workbook in the series. For more information on other workbooks, pl. visit www.pendrawings.me/workbooks.

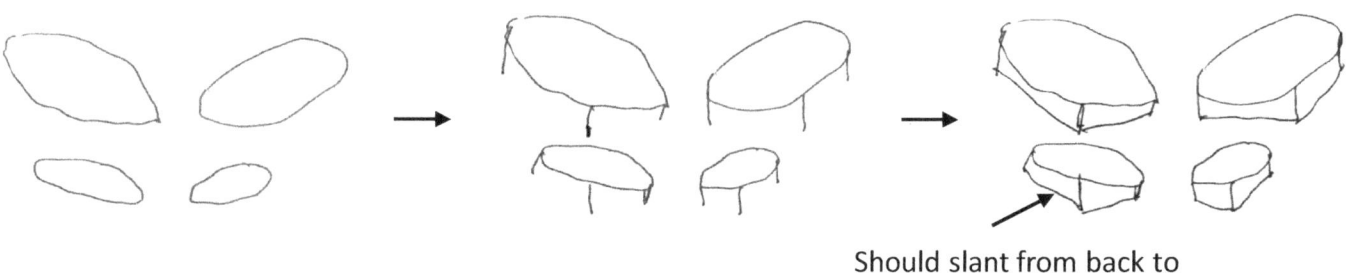

Should slant from back to front

Start by drawing such slanted ovals for the top of stones.

Next drop lines from the edges and somewhere in the center as shown above. Make center line longer.

Connect the bottom of lines to define sides.

Adding Stones as Foreground Elements, Continued:

Vol. 3 of the series contains full details on drawing stones. For more information, Pl. visit www.pendrawings.me/workbooks.

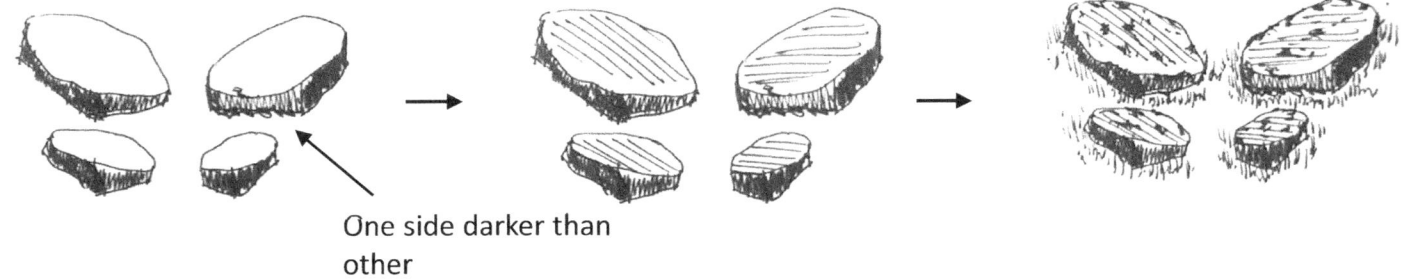

One side darker than other

Darken the sides. Make one side darker than other.

Use parallel lines to define the surface contour of the top.

Add tapered crevices and edge irregularities to bring out the feel of stone.

Drawing Group of Stones:

To draw group of stones, draw stones in front first. Then add stones behind by partially hiding them by starting their outline from edges of stones in front. Vol. 3 of the workbook series contains full details on drawing stones. For more information, Pl. visit www.pendrawings.me/workbooks.

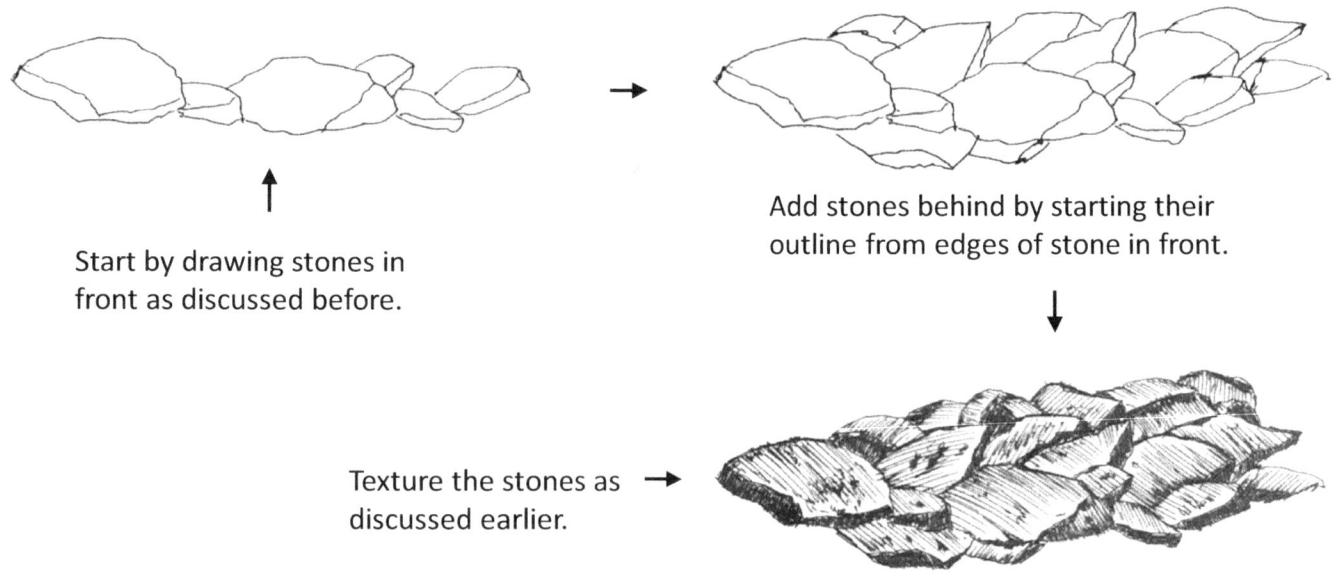

Start by drawing stones in front as discussed before.

Add stones behind by starting their outline from edges of stone in front.

Texture the stones as discussed earlier.

Activity: Drawing Stones:

Texture the following stone outline. Add more and texture them as discussed earlier.

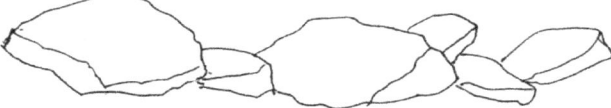

Landscapes with Stones:

We have seen many landscapes with stones so far and that speaks to their versatility in giving visual interest to the foreground. They can be used very effectively with other elements. Landscape just with stones as main visual element is also very appealing as seen below.

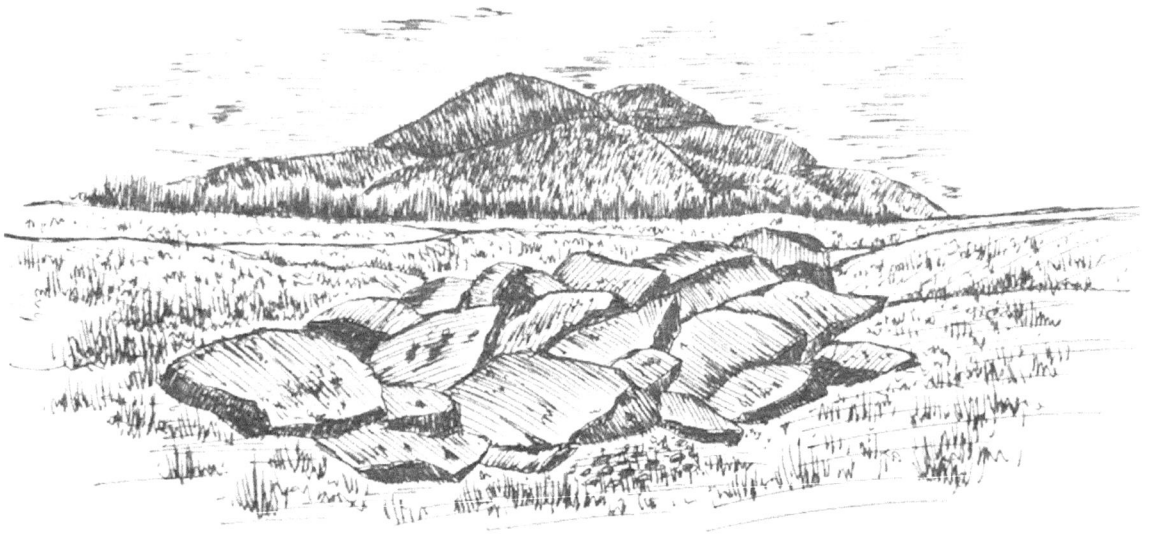

Once you learn to draw group of stones, such simple landscapes in limitless variations can be easily drawn from imagination.

Drawing Snow Covered Pine Trees:

Snow covered pine trees are another wonderful addition to any winter landscapes. By implying the white of paper as snow, they can be easily drawn with use of right stroke. They are again covered in detail in Vol. 3 of the series. For more information, Pl. visit www.pendrawings.me/workbooks.

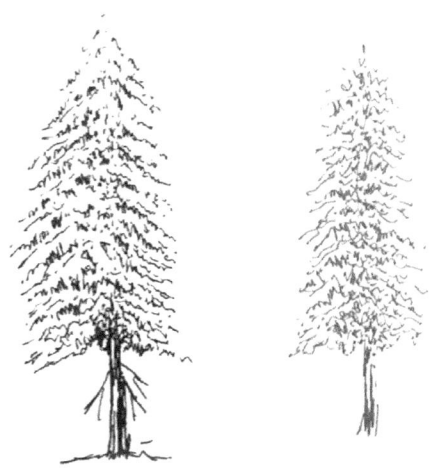

Notice how irregular strokes are used to indicate needles not covered by snow. Such combination of irregular dark and white of paper conveys feel of snow.

By irregularly defining edges and leaving the center irregularly white, feel of snow covered pine trees can be evoked.

Close up of Stroke Used.

Landscapes with Snow Covered Pine Trees:

Once you learn to draw snow covered pine trees, very pleasing winter landscapes can be easily drawn from imagination. Draw such trees at different distances to give depth. Bare winter trees and other elements can be added as well..

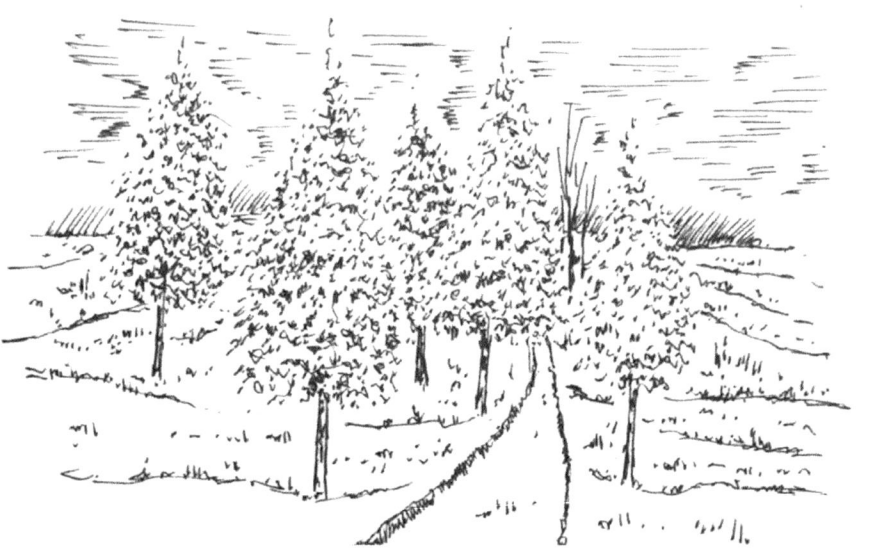

Ground is also lightly textured to bring out the feel of snow.

Activity: Drawing Snow Covered Pine Trees:

Use the space below to draw snow covered pine trees as discussed earlier.

Another drawing with snow covered pine trees. When combined with bare winter trees, they really set the winter mood.

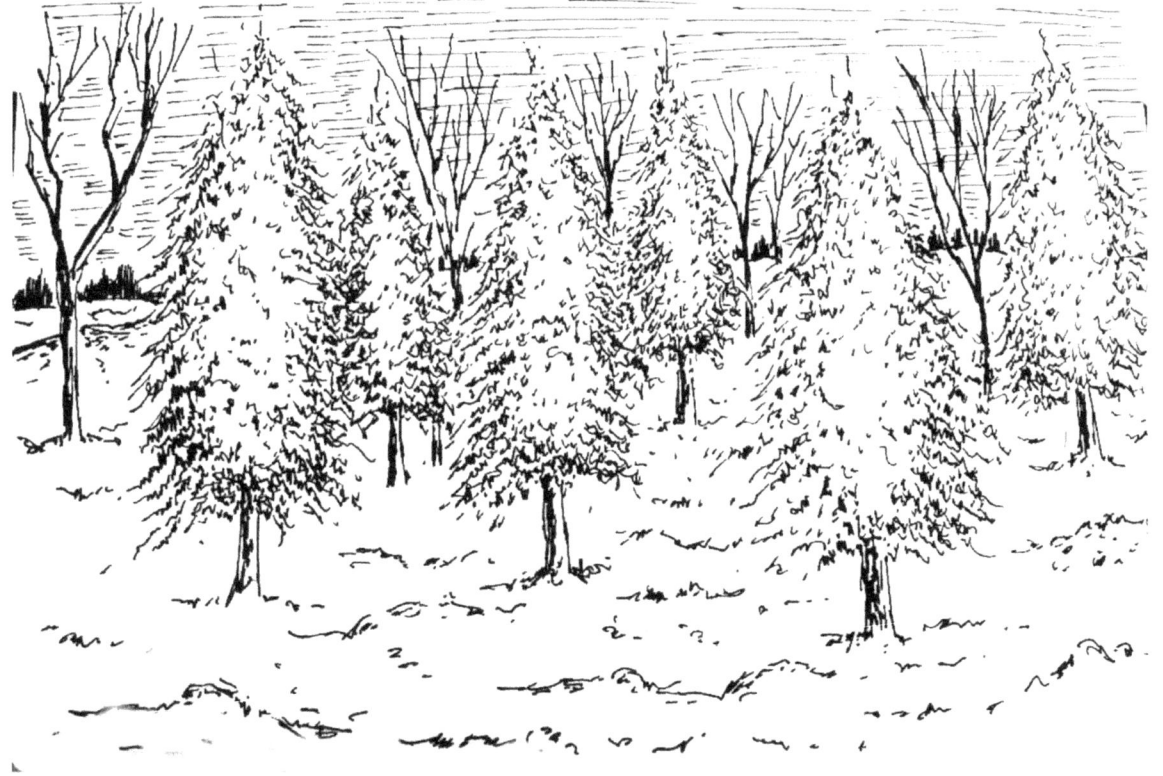

Adding Wooden Posts:

Weathered Wooden posts are a great addition in the foreground. They add a rustic charm to any landscapes and are very easy to draw. Drawing them is covered in detail in vol 1-2 workbook in the series. Please visit www.pendrawings.me/workbooks for more information.

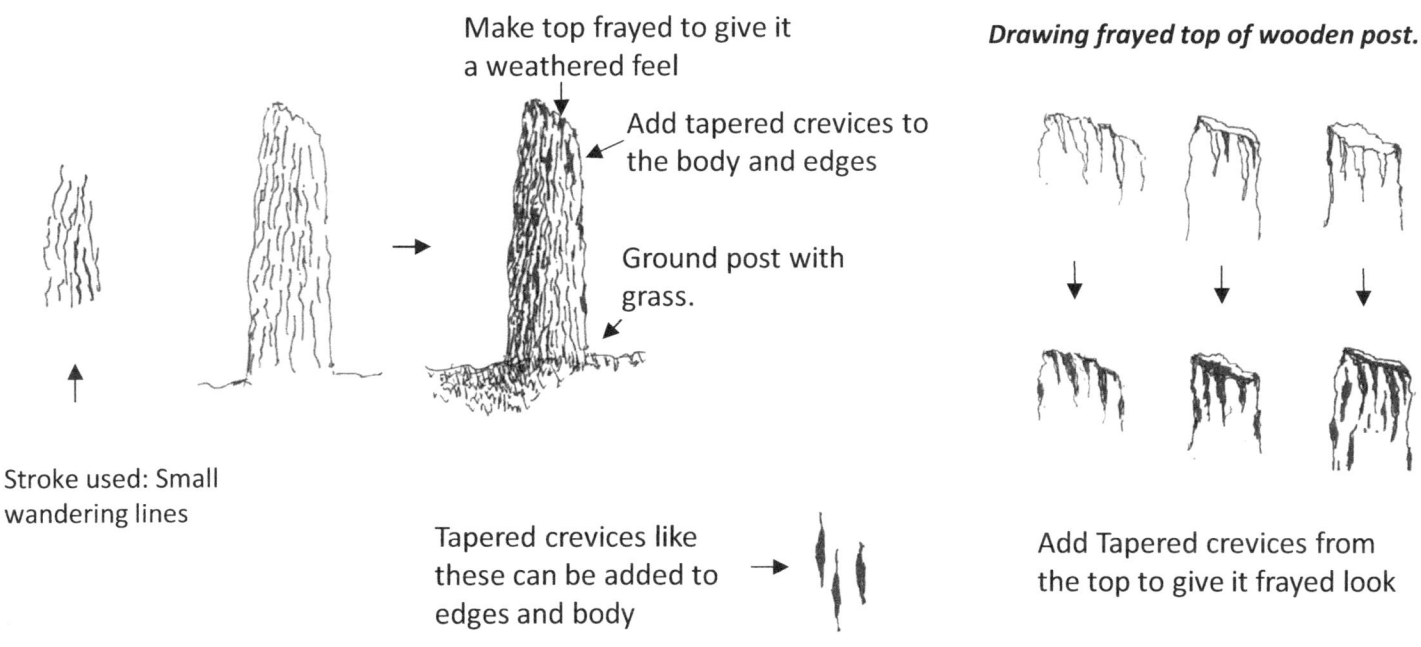

Adding Wooden Posts, Continued:

Far away or smaller wooden posts can be drawn by simply darkening one side irregularly as shown below. Always keep in mind that size of a drawing dictates the level of details it will have. For posts closer to viewer, add more details using stroke discussed on last page. For smaller far away posts, use the following approach.

← Start by drawing the outline as shown.

Same technique can be used for drawing receding posts.

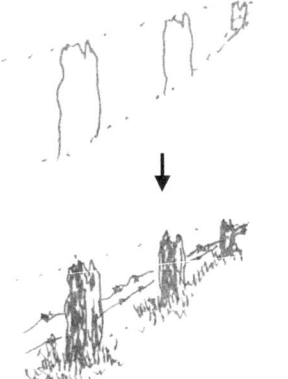

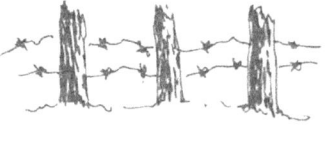

← Darken one end in a zagged manner to bring out their roundness.

Activity: Texturing Wooden Posts:

Practice texturing wooden posts below. Draw some of your own and texture them.

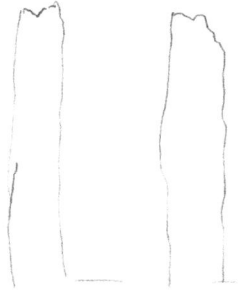
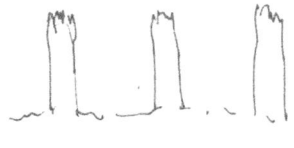
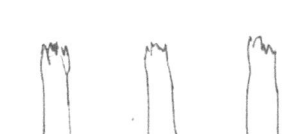

Landscapes with Wooden Posts:

We have seen some examples of landscapes with wooden posts earlier. Following is another example. An old falling wooden fence along with group of stones constitutes the foreground.

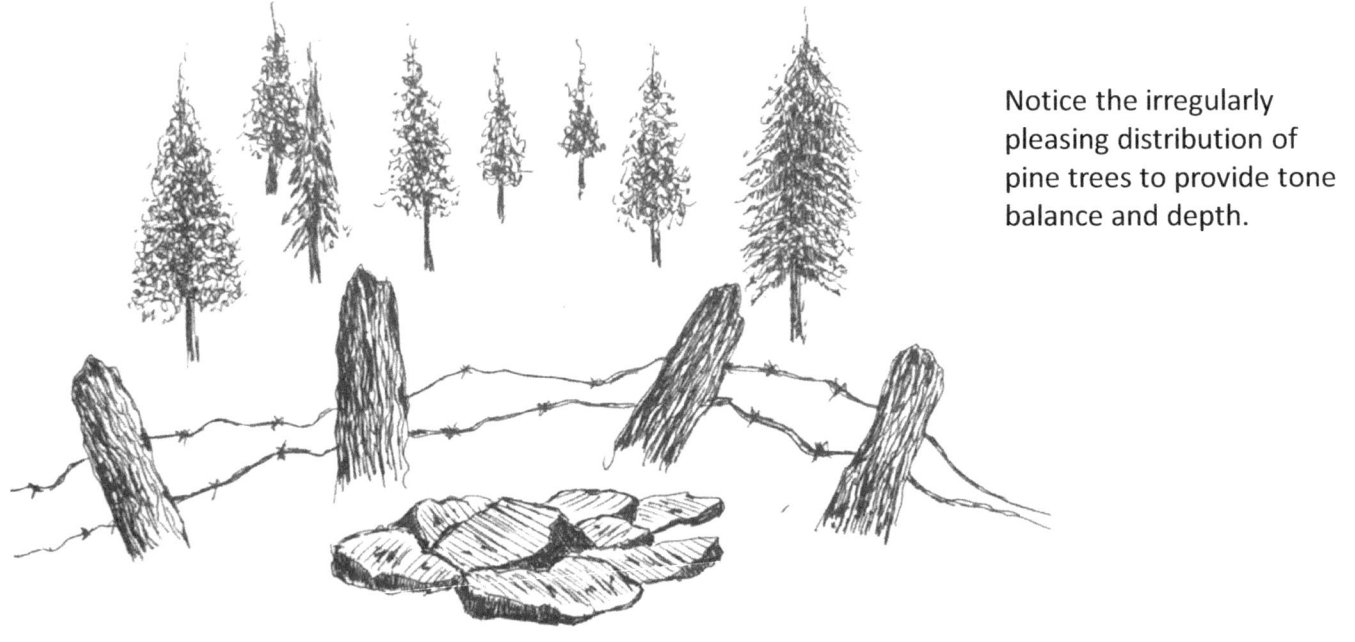

Notice the irregularly pleasing distribution of pine trees to provide tone balance and depth.

Landscapes with Wooden Posts, Continued:

Plain lines are next added. Note that different plain lines could have been added to give a very different feel.

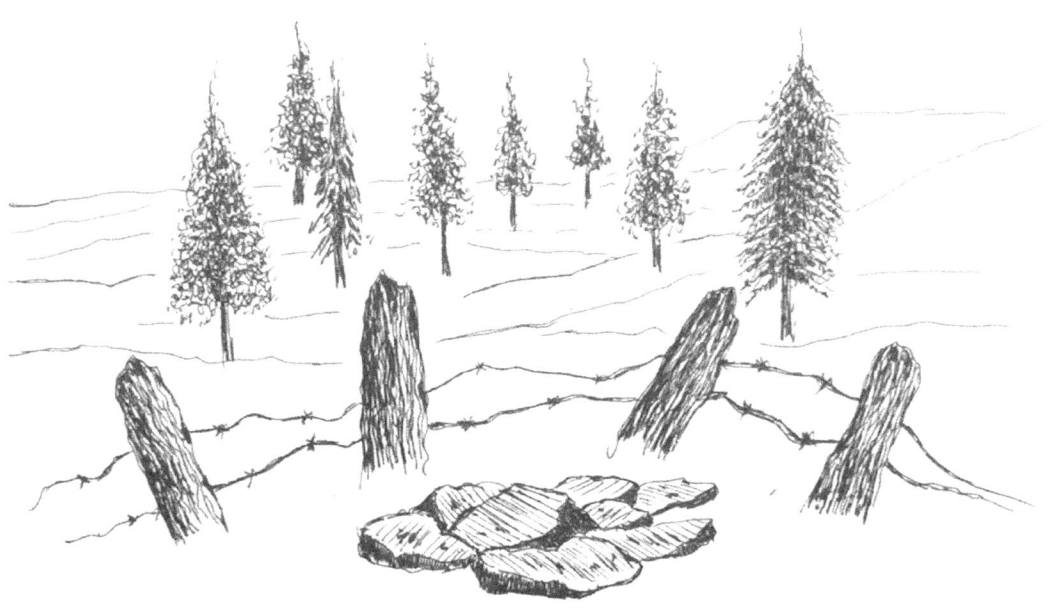

Combination of diminishing size of trees and plains in distance adds to perception of depth in the drawing.

Landscapes with Wooden Posts, Continued:

Ground and other background elements are added to finish the drawing.

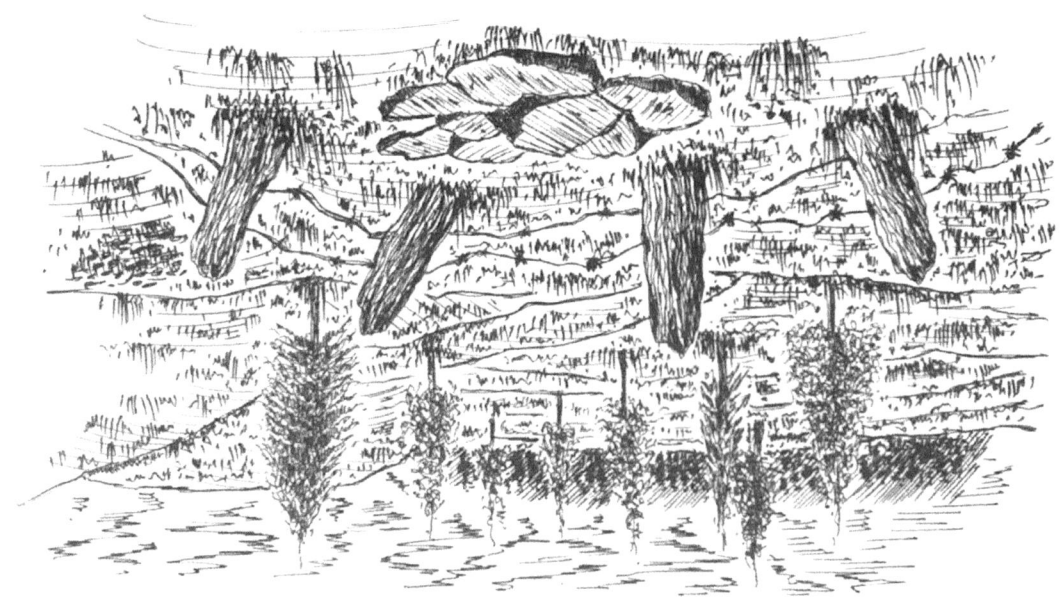

Notice how wooden posts and stones adds foreground appeal in the drawing.

Size Matters:

As I have mentioned before, drawing at a bigger size allows more elements and more details to be added. At a smaller size trying to add more stuff just results in dark mess. In last few examples, we looked at drawings at relatively larger size with more elements. But it is also fun to do small quick drawings as shown below. Here details are not present, but by using good combination of elements and interesting plains, they can be made quite appealing

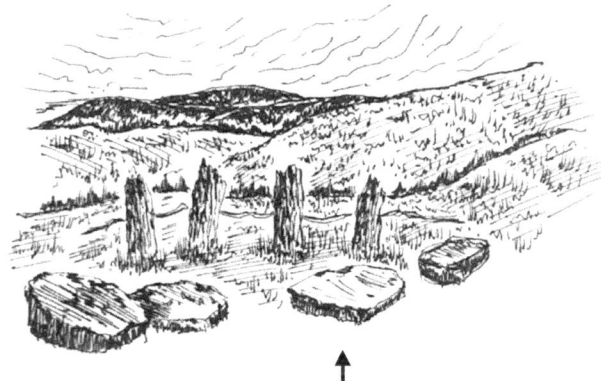

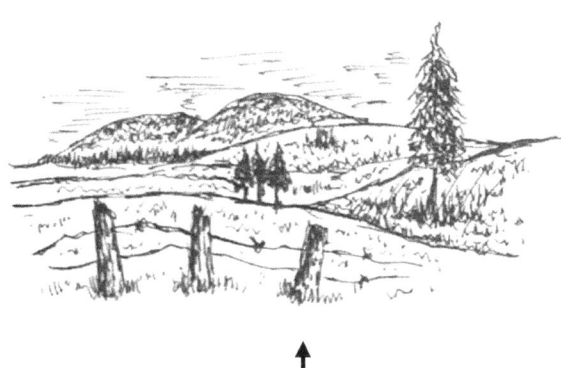

↑

Notice the layers of tonal contrast above. Stones and posts are darker with lighter middle ground between followed by darker distant hills and lighter clouds. Such alternating tones creates visual interest and makes a drawing attractive. This is especially important for small drawings with less details.

↑

Here again the ground is left light to provide a 'canvas' for other elements.

Small Landscapes, More Examples:

Following are some more example of small sized landscapes. As you can see, they can be quite interesting with combination of tonal contrast, perception of depth and interesting plains arrangement. Try one of your own.

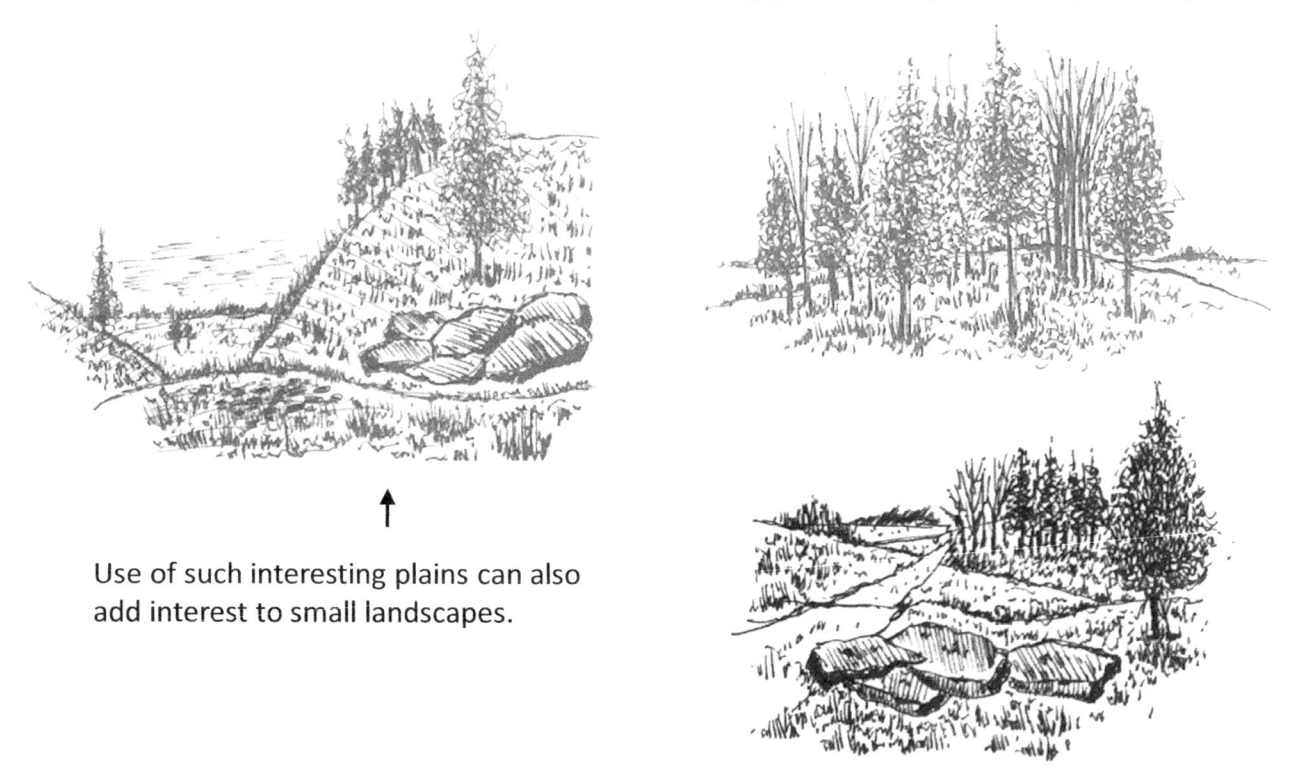

↑

Use of such interesting plains can also add interest to small landscapes.

Drawing Deciduous Trees:

Deciduous trees are also very common elements in a landscape. Drawing them is covered extensively in vol 1-2 of the workbook series. Here we will learn how to draw them at smaller size with few details. For full in depth discussion on drawing trees in detail, pl. consult vol 1-2 of the workbook series. You can find more information at www.pendrawings.me/workbooks.

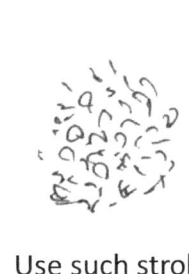

Use such strokes to indicate foliage.

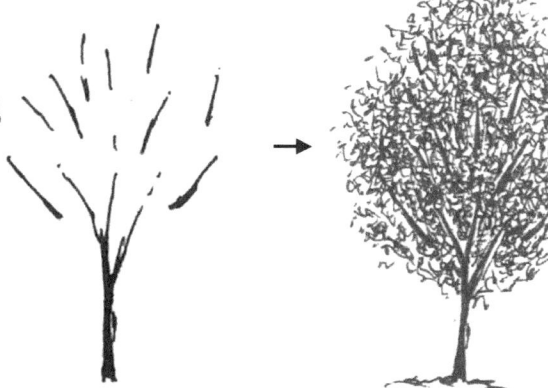

Draw trunk and broken branches outline using solid tapered dark.

Next add foliage in between. Keep small white between branch and foliage.

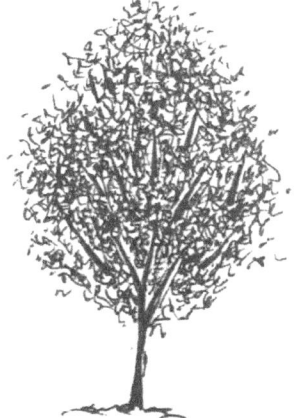

Young trees and trees of any shape and size can be drawn by using appropriate 'skeleton' structure.

Drawing Deciduous Trees, Continued:

Following are some more examples. In a drawing with many trees, use different shapes and sizes to add visual interest.

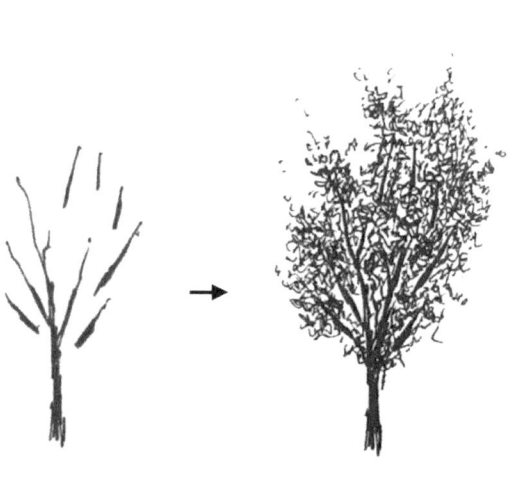

Here is another example. Such asymmetrical trees are more interesting than symmetrical dome shaped trees.

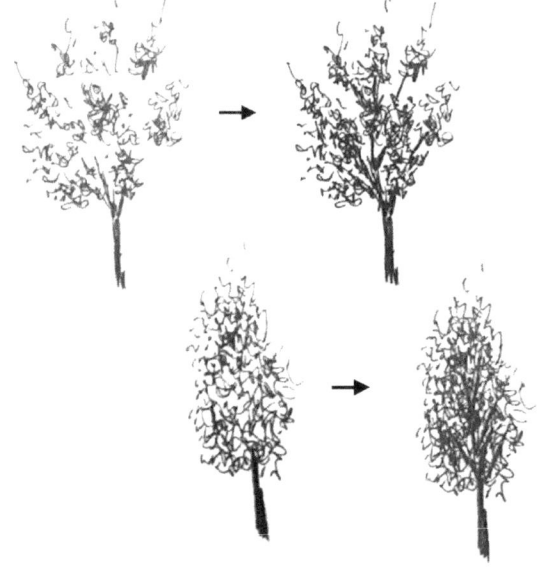

In an alternate approach, foliage masses can be drawn first and then connected.

Drawing Landscapes with Deciduous Trees:

We earlier saw how to incorporate pine trees and bare winter trees in a landscapes. Deciduous trees can be incorporated in a similar manner. Use pleasing distribution at different depths to make it visually inviting. Other foreground elements like stones and wooden posts can be added as well..

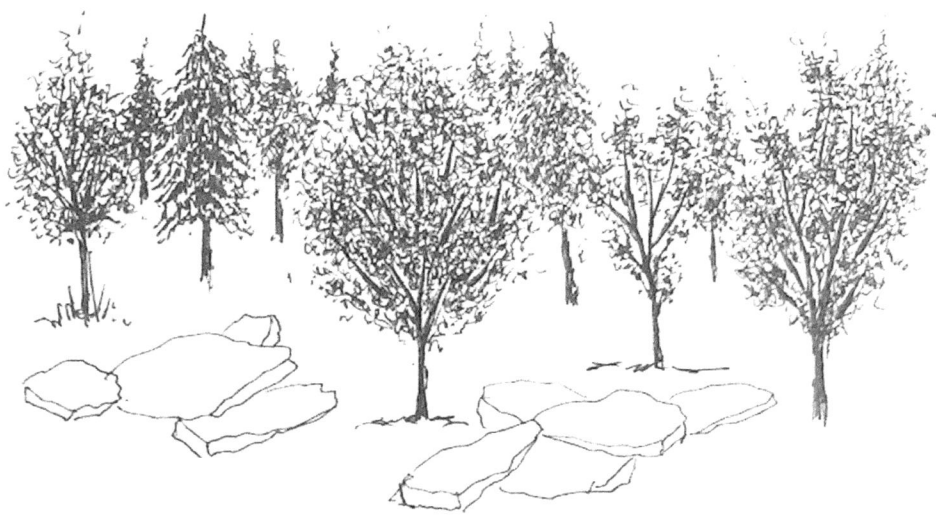

As discussed before, start by laying down main elements. Deciduous and Pine tress are used here along with stones in the foreground.

Drawing Landscapes with Deciduous Trees, Continued:

Finishe as discussed before. Again notice that ground is kept lighter to contrast with darker tone of trees. This creates a clear visual separation and makes trees the focal point. Such tonal separation is very important in pen and ink drawing.

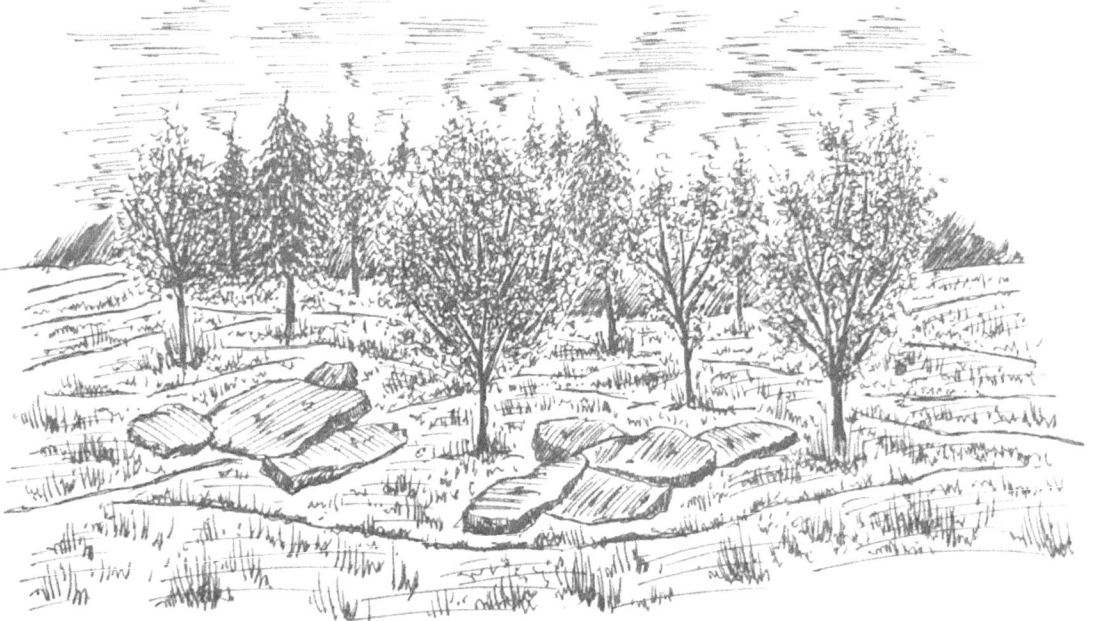

Using Interesting Plains:

As discussed before, plain lines essentially define the arrangement of ground. In the first drawing below, different plains can be defined. I could have draw a flat receding plains like in some previous landscapes, but I chose more angular right side as seen in the second drawing. This gives more visual interest compared to a flat ground. Experiment with such different choices in your attempts.

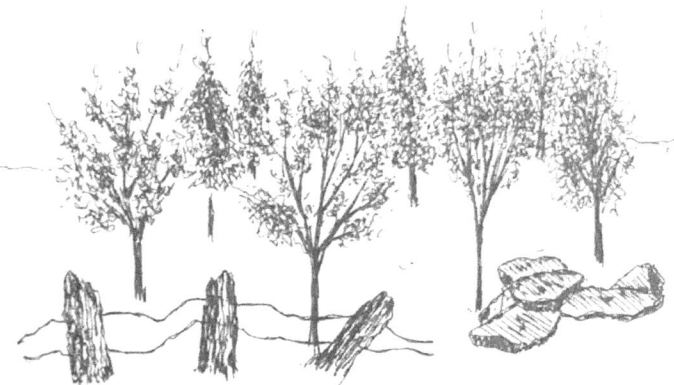

Leave some white where you intend the plain lines to run through.

Conceptualize the landscape in your mind and draw other elements appropriately. Draw them at different heights, distances etc. based on how you intend to draw the plains.

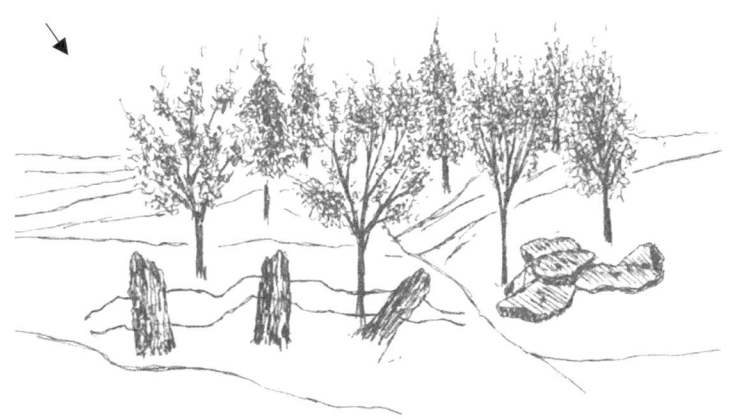

Using Interesting Plains, Continued:

Here is the finished drawing from previous discussion. Notice how asymmetry in plains adds interest and appeal to the drawing. Notice that ground is again kept lighter to contrast with other darker elements.

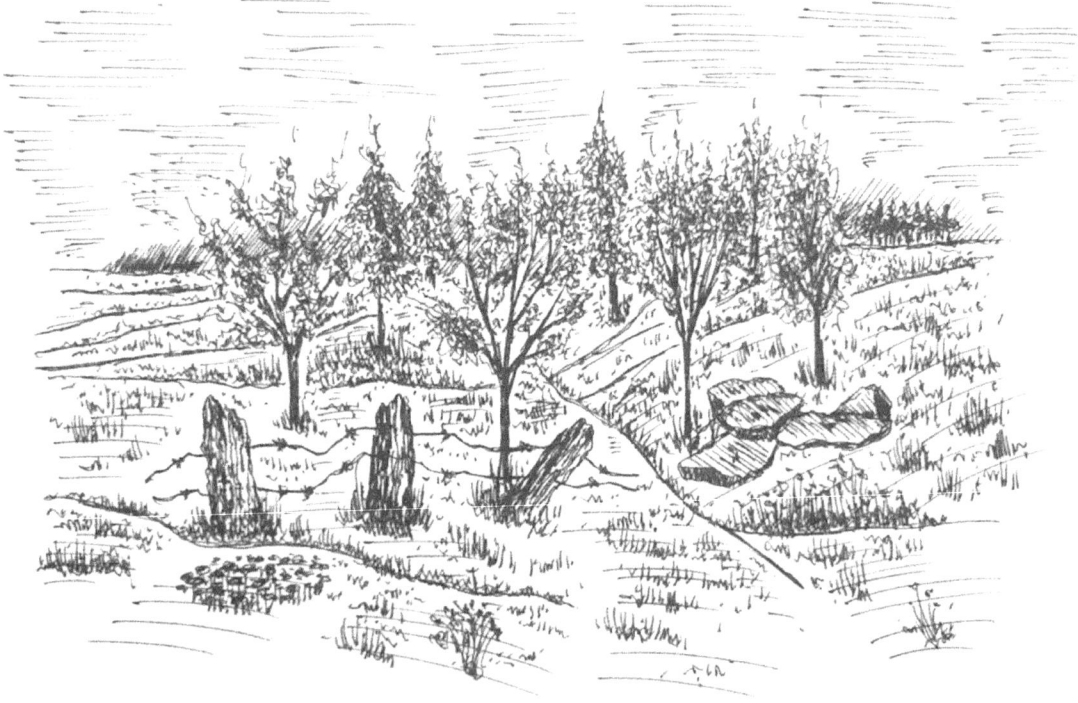

Keeping Visual Separation:

Higher density of trees that are behind each other is more visually appealing. In this case, be very careful to maintain visual separation between foreground and background trees. Use a very small sliver of white or light tone at the meeting area between trees to maintain their separation. Study the close up from the last drawing below. Notice how there is small light area for trees to stand apart.

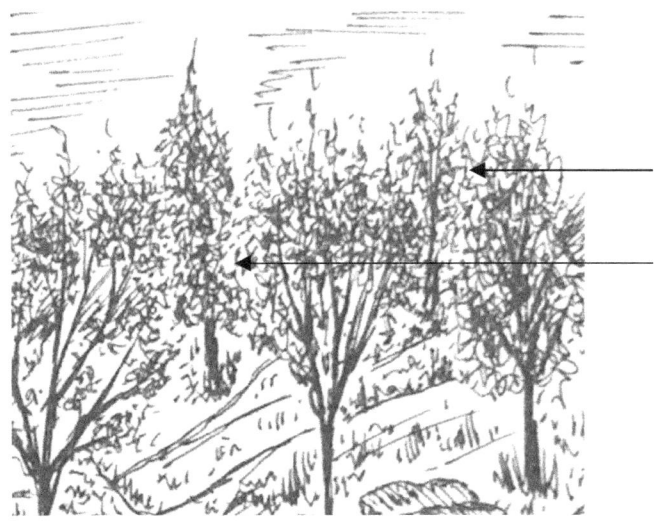

Notice these lighter areas that visually separate trees. Lot of this comes with practice. Initially, draw trees far apart to physically distance them. As you add more density, use such light tone or white between overlapping elements to maintain their visual separation.

Alternate Technique for Drawing Deciduous Trees:

Angular parallel lines and technique that was used to draw distant element can be also used to draw trees. They give a bit 'hazy' feel to trees are more appropriate when drawing trees at a distance.

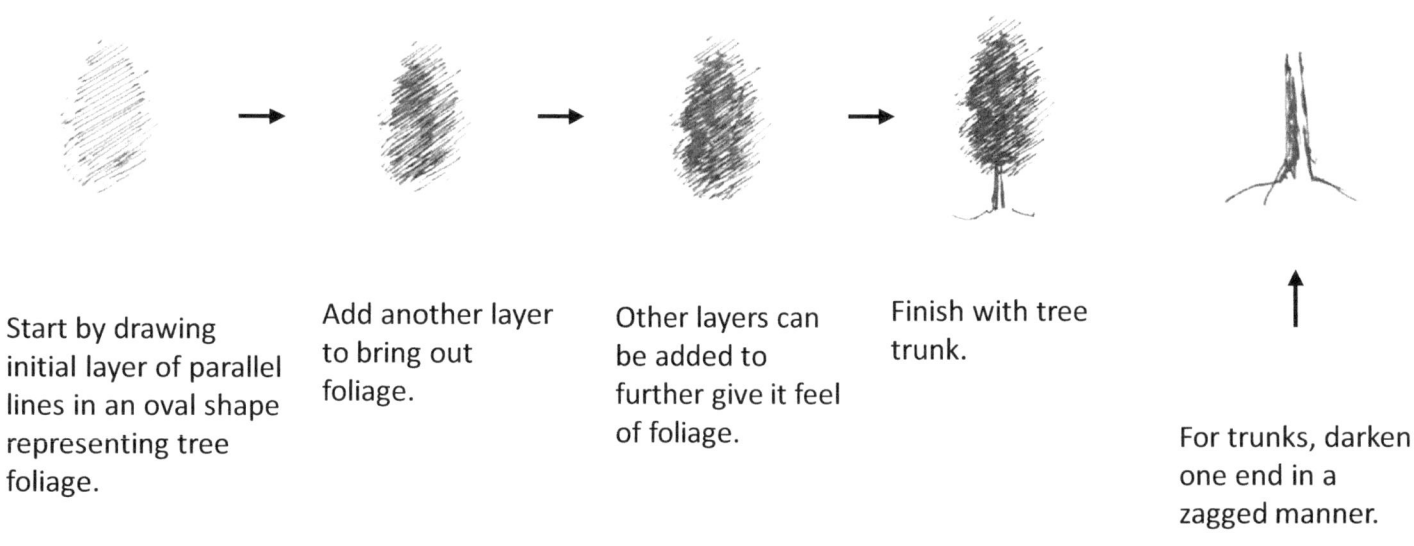

Start by drawing initial layer of parallel lines in an oval shape representing tree foliage.

Add another layer to bring out foliage.

Other layers can be added to further give it feel of foliage.

Finish with tree trunk.

For trunks, darken one end in a zagged manner.

Small Sized Landscapes with Trees:

Technique discussed on last page for drawing trees is very quick to do and is ideally suited for drawing quick small sized landscapes with trees. As the size of trees is small in these drawings, they work well as seen below. For bigger drawings where tree foliage need to be depicted, used the foliage technique.

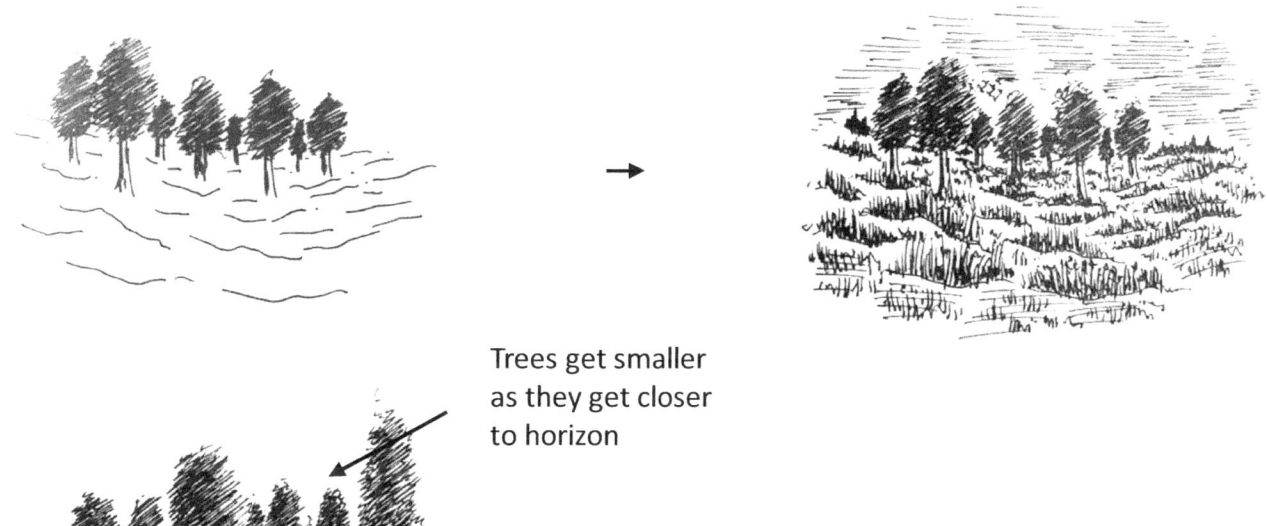

Trees get smaller as they get closer to horizon

In the previous pages, we covered in detail the steps for creating simple pleasing landscapes from your imagination based on composition presented in the beginning. Different options for these steps were presented and discussed.

We will now further look at some other ways in which different steps in this composition can be done. They create a different feel for the drawing and can be effectively combined with other techniques that have been presented to create even more variation and interest in your drawings.

My aim is to give you a 'toolkit' of different strokes and techniques that you can mix and match and adopt in different ways by using your creativity in your drawings to create a different one from your imagination anytime. Techniques presented next will further add to your 'toolkit'.

Another Way of Texturing Ground:

Here is another way to texture ground. In this technique, 'ground imperfection lines' are drawn from foreground to horizon. These imperfection lines gives indication of ground irregularities. Receding Foliage is drawn on them to further bring out the imperfections. This gives a very pleasing feel to the ground.

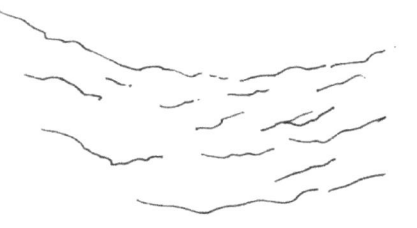

Start by drawing these 'organic' imperfection lines in front of the horizon. Make them smaller near the horizon and increase them towards the foreground.

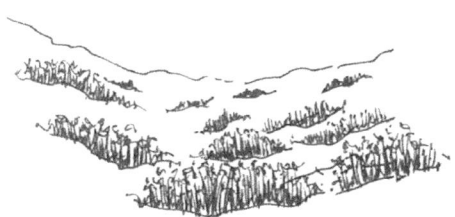

Texture them with foliage as discussed next.

Another Way of Texturing Ground, Continued:

Use different sizes and spread the imperfections lines to make them visually appealing. This technique is also discussed in detail in other volumes in the series in the context of drawing larger sized landscapes.

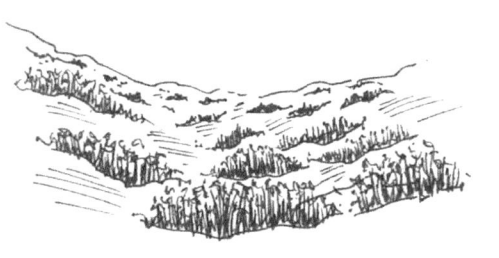

Very small imperfections near the horizon can be added further to give more depth. Contour lines as discussed before can also be used in the white between the imperfections to give ground definition

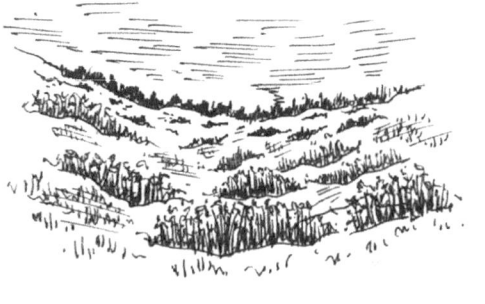

Add grass to contour lines and finish as before.

Adding Foliage to Imperfection Lines:

As seen on last page, drawing foliage on imperfection lines really helps to bring out their contours and gives a pleasing feel to the ground. Use following steps to add foliage to them. Remember to make it smaller closer to horizon.

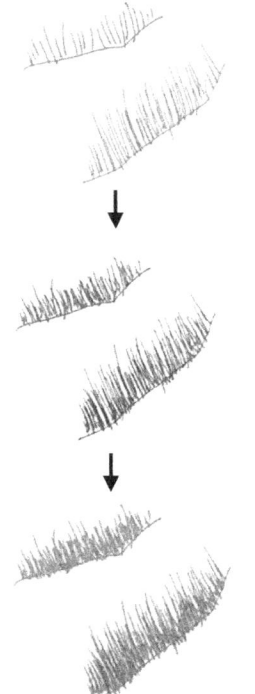

Start by adding such curved lines on the imperfection line. Taper it at start and end.

Add another set of lines to darken the bottom.

Bottom can be further darkened with another set of lines.

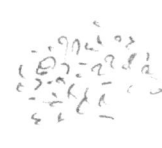 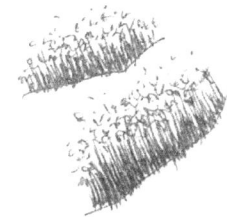

Tick marks as shown can be used to give indication of leaves etc. on the top as well.

Another Example of Previous Technique:

Following is another example of technique discussed last. By using interesting shapes, sizes and distribution for ground imperfection lines, very pleasing variations can be easily drawn from imagination.

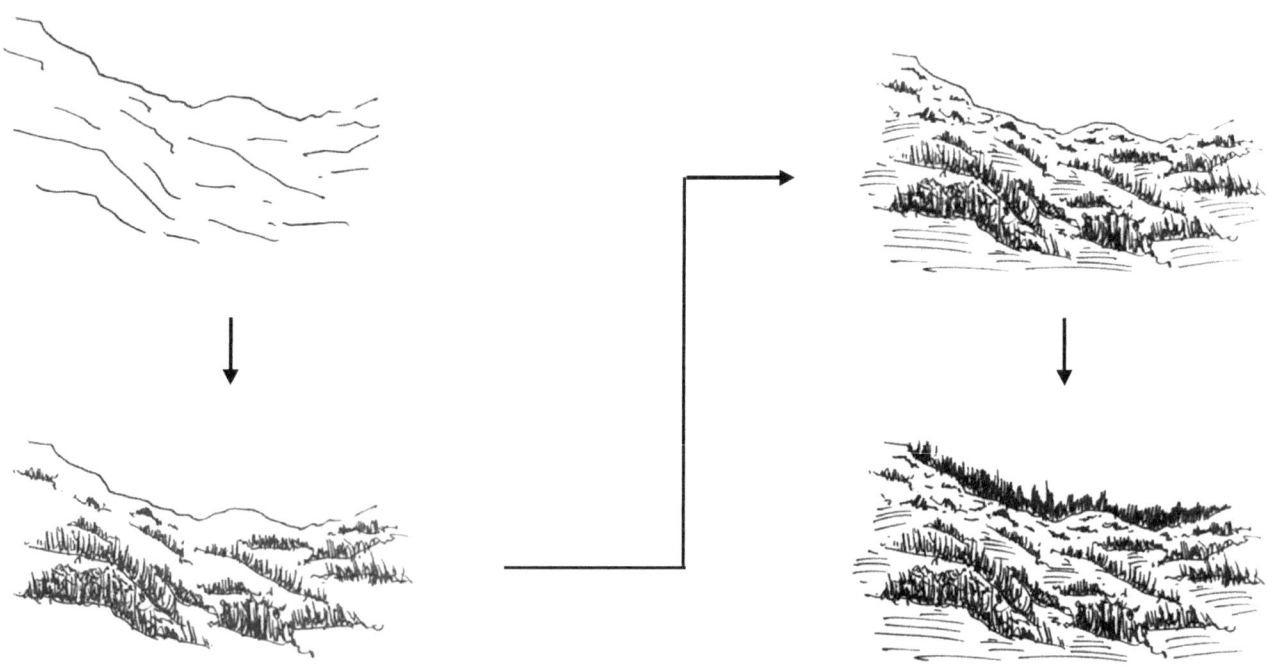

Yet Another Example of Previous Technique:

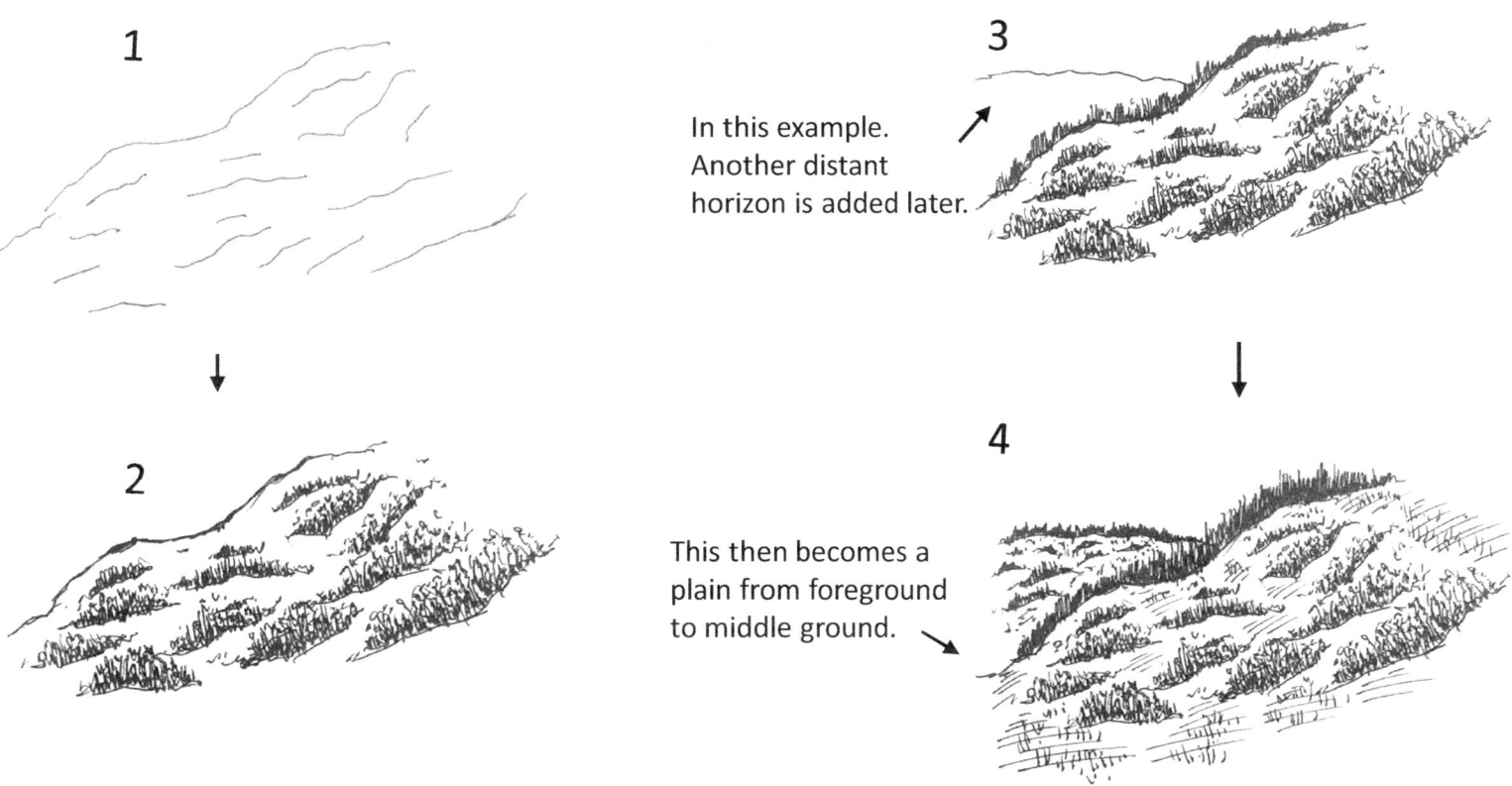

Another Way of Texturing Ground:

This is a different technique for giving ground definition. It uses simple lines and doesn't require use of parallel lines like earlier technique.

In this technique, lines like these are used to give surface definition.

This technique gives a different pleasing feel to the ground. Use the direction and density of such lines to give the desired feel for surface contour.

Use such small lines near horizon to give it additional texture.

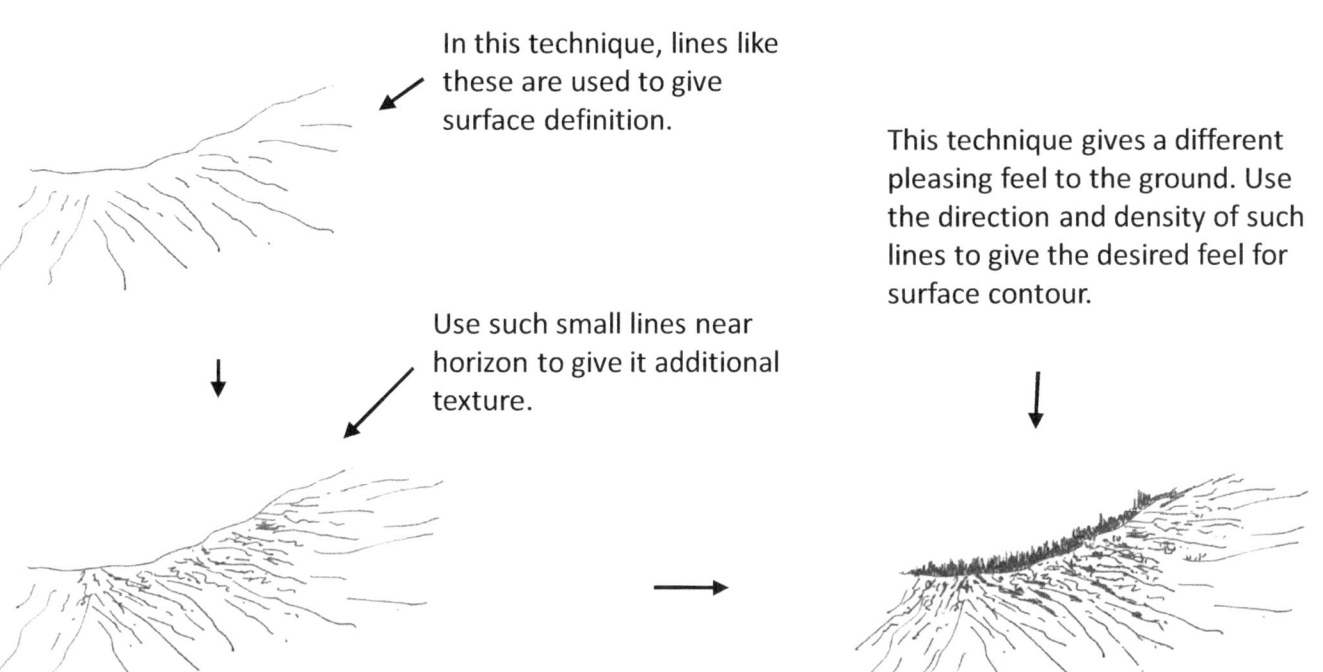

Another Example:

Following is another example of texturing ground using this technique.

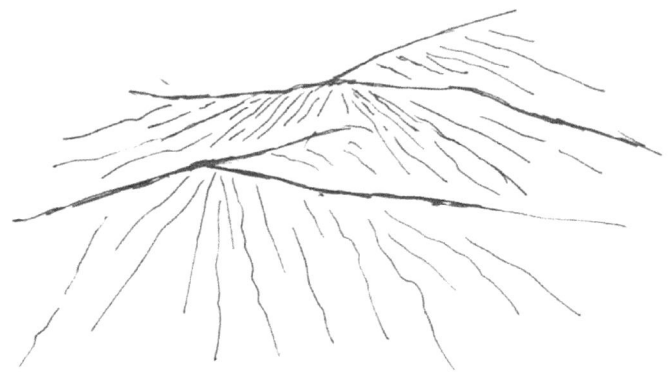

Yet Another Way of Texturing Ground:

Another way is to draw grass, wild flowers etc. using simple strokes to give a pleasing indication of ground. Study the kind of strokes shown below. By using them in different ways along with variation in tone, you can create a pleasing indication of ground covered in grass and flowers.

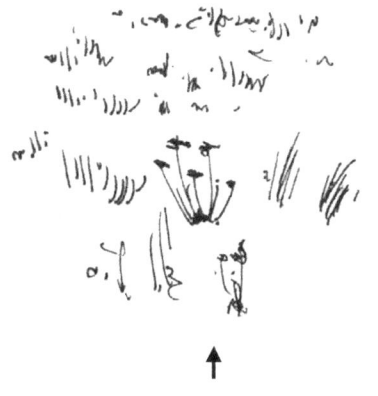

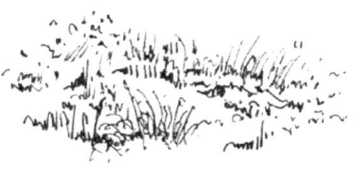

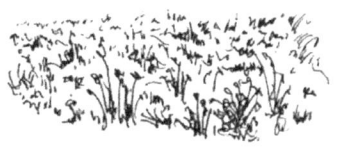

Enlarged view of kind of strokes that can be used. There is no limit to them. Create and use your strokes of this kind.

By using such strokes, a pleasant indication of ground can be given. Study how small variation in tone is used to add depth and interest in the drawing.

Yet Another Way of Texturing Ground, Continued:

Following are some more examples. There is really no limit to the different feel for ground that can be given this way.

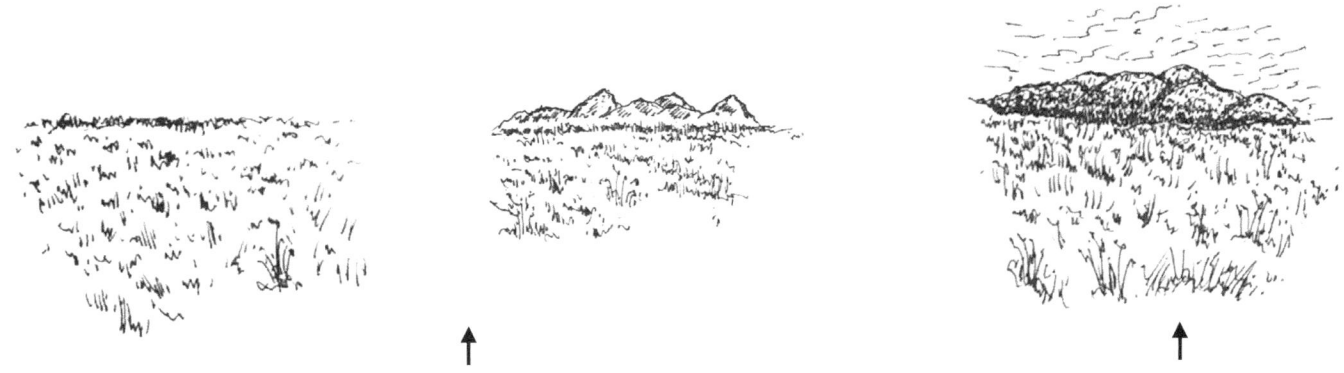

Some more examples. The white of paper is part of texture. Don't cover it all but leave some white to contrast against what you have drawn.

Draw grass/flowers near viewer larger and ones closer to horizon much smaller due to perspective. This adds to depth. Relative difference in their size will convey the distance between them.

Comparison of Ground Cover Techniques:

Here is a side by side look at different ways of indicating ground that we covered so far. Notice how each approach gives a different feel and can be combined with other steps. Indeed with practice, you will develop your own such techniques.

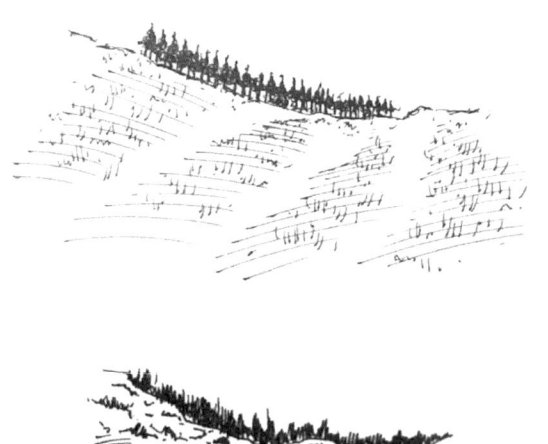

When you come across a pen and ink drawing, try to understand how the ground is textured in it. What strokes are used and what is the manner of their use. By such study, you will be able to further increase your 'toolkit' of techniques.

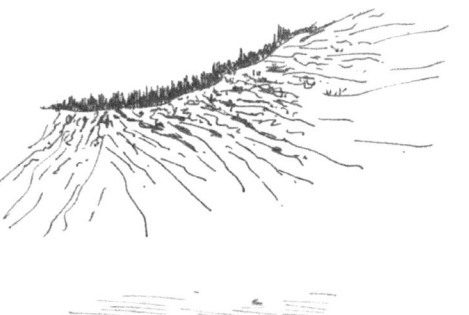

Combining Different Ground Texturing Techniques:

Different techniques discussed for texturing ground creates different feel for the ground. They can be combined to create ground texture with more varied feel as shown below. Try a combination of your own.

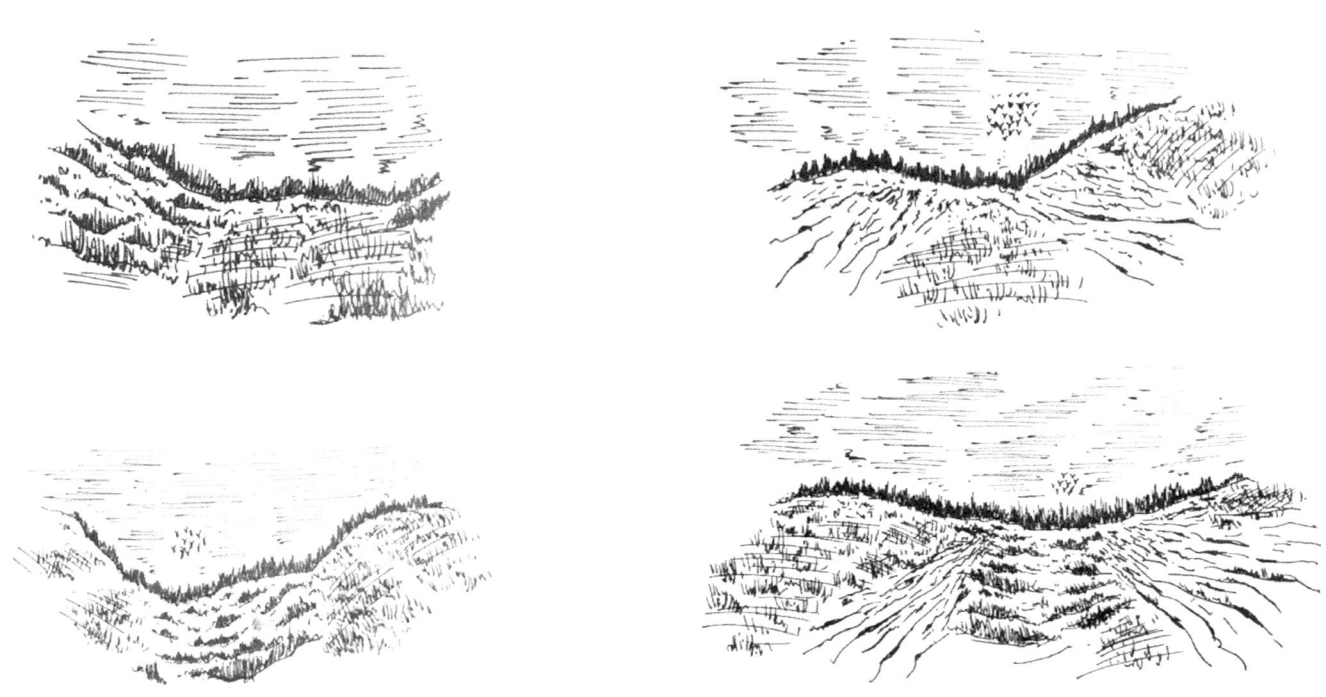

Adding Zagged Foreground:

Following is a nice way to add further interest in the drawing. Here, a zagged foreground is added against which the distant elements are drawn. Use of such foreground adds a different feel to the drawing.

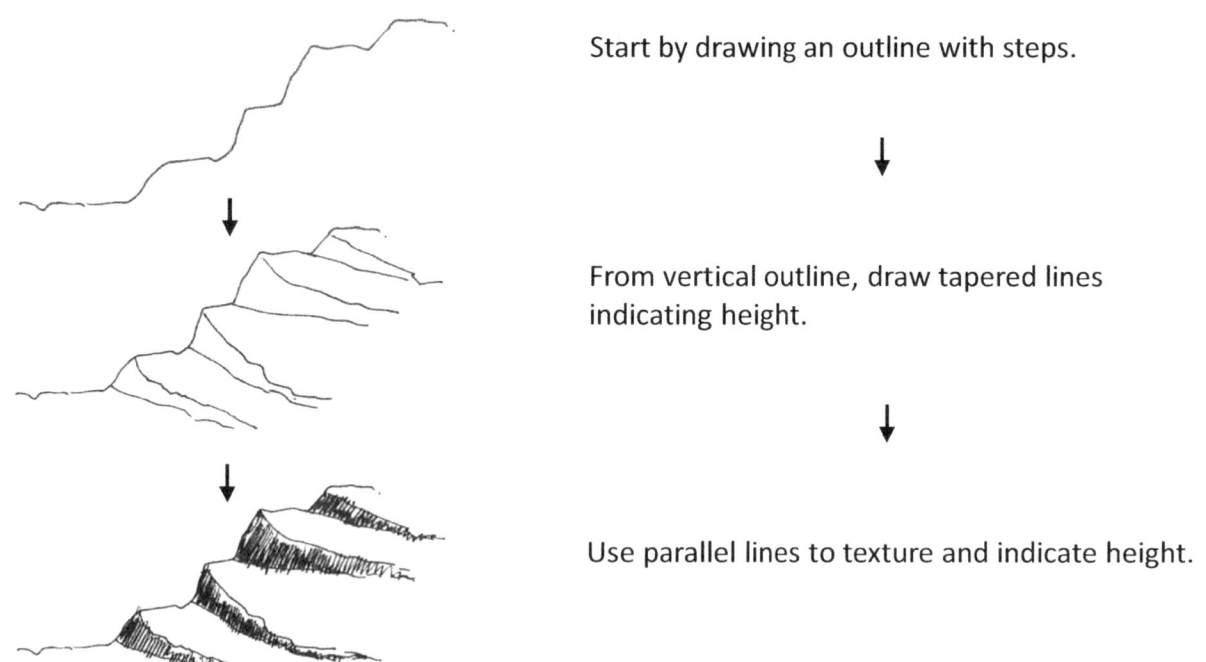

Start by drawing an outline with steps.

From vertical outline, draw tapered lines indicating height.

Use parallel lines to texture and indicate height.

Adding Zagged Foreground, Continued:

Foreground also becomes a focal point using this approach. The roughness of zagged edges contrasts well with use of more mellow edges for background elements.

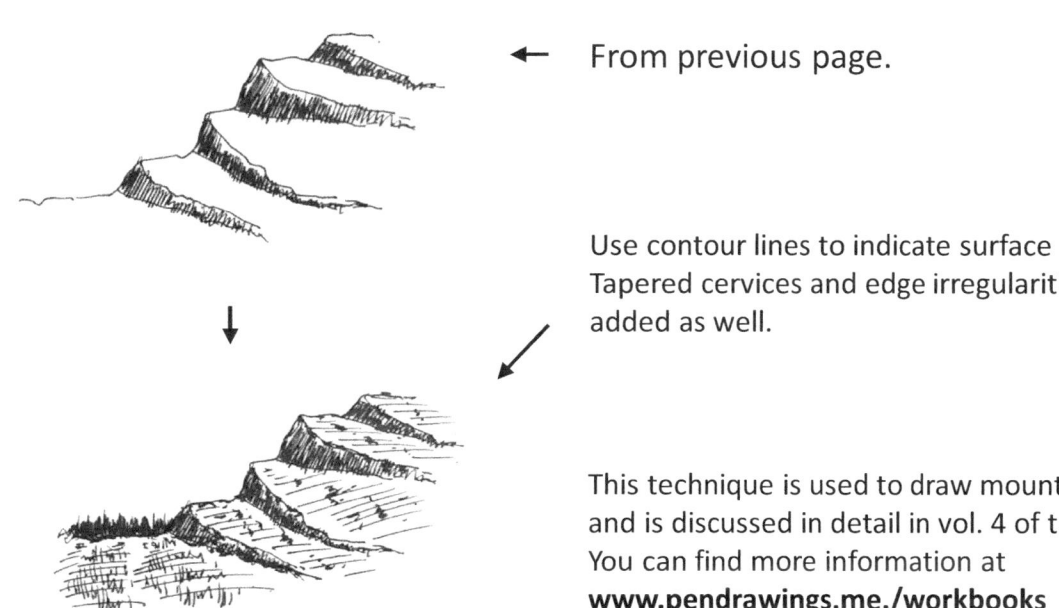

← From previous page.

Use contour lines to indicate surface definition. Tapered cervices and edge irregularities can be added as well.

This technique is used to draw mountains as well and is discussed in detail in vol. 4 of the series. You can find more information at
www.pendrawings.me./workbooks

Activity: Drawing Zagged Foreground:

Complete the following zagged foregrounds as discussed earlier.

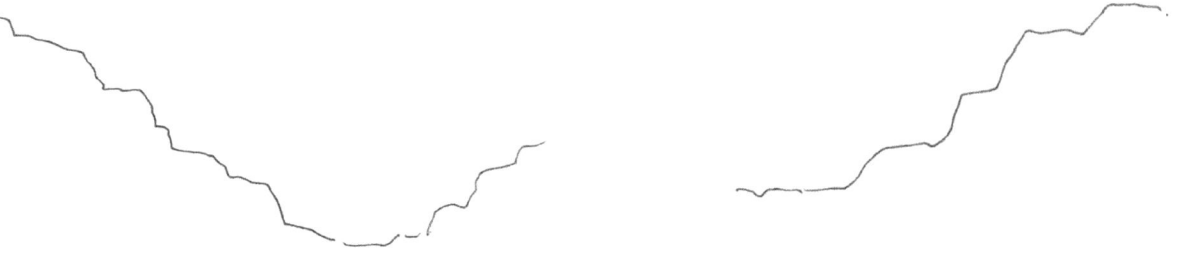

Some More Examples of Zagged Foreground:

This is a very flexible technique and such interesting zagged foreground can be easily drawn to add more visual interest to any drawing.

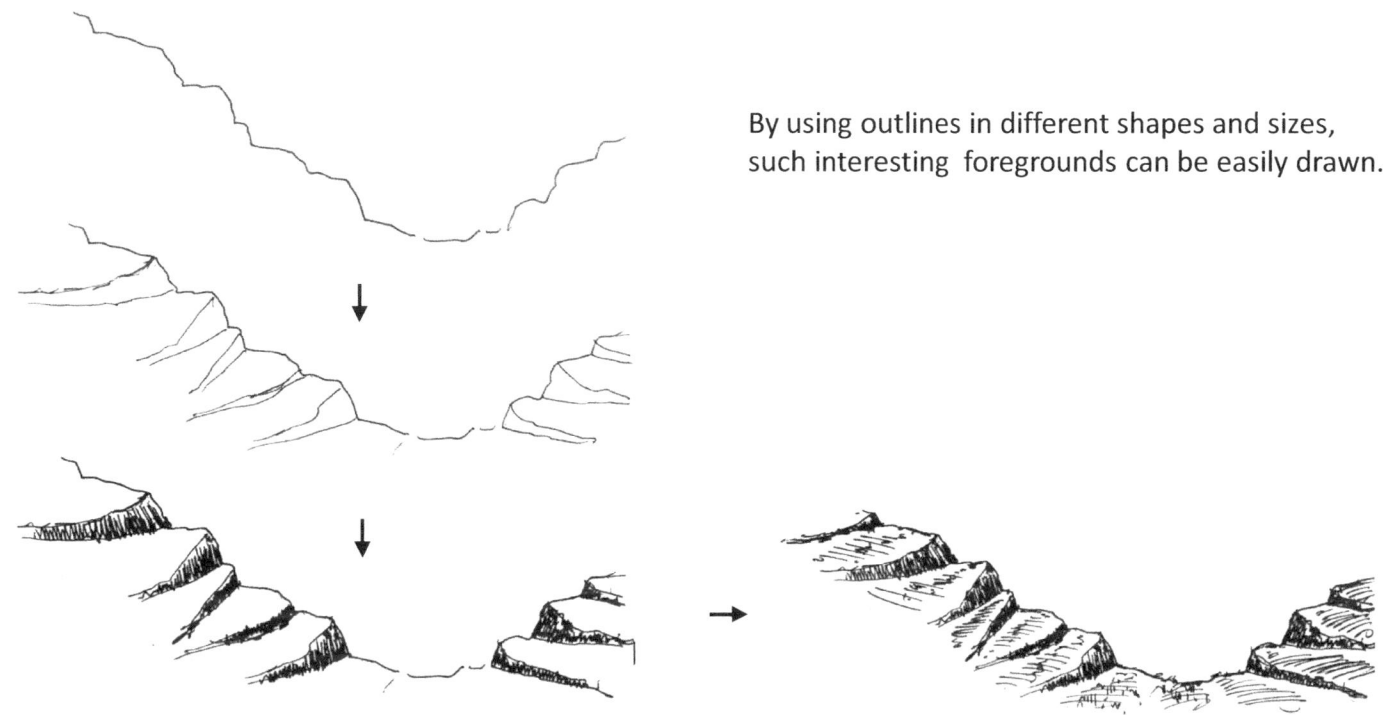

By using outlines in different shapes and sizes, such interesting foregrounds can be easily drawn.

Landscapes with Zagged Foreground:

.

Following are some examples where zagged foreground is used to create visual interest.

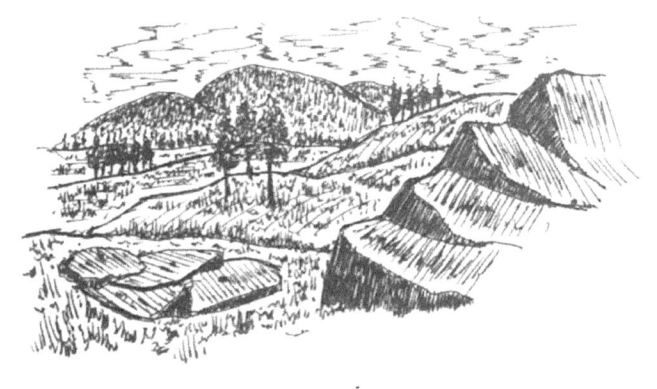 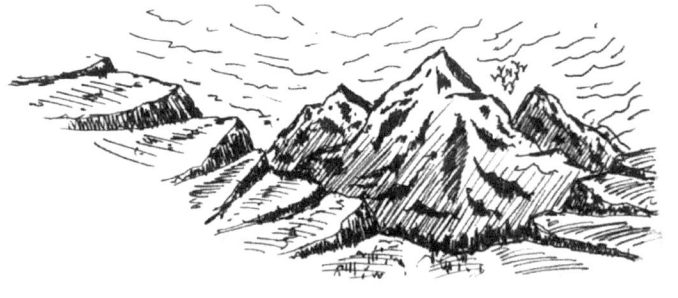

Lighter tone should be used in the vicinity of zagged foreground as its vertical edges are darker in tone.

Here zagged foreground extends to both sides with a notion of horizon in the center against which distant element is drawn.

Creating More Interesting Plains:

Instead of steep vertical sides, the technique of zagged foreground can be used to create mellow sides as well. This can further be extended to other plains to create ground with more visual interest.

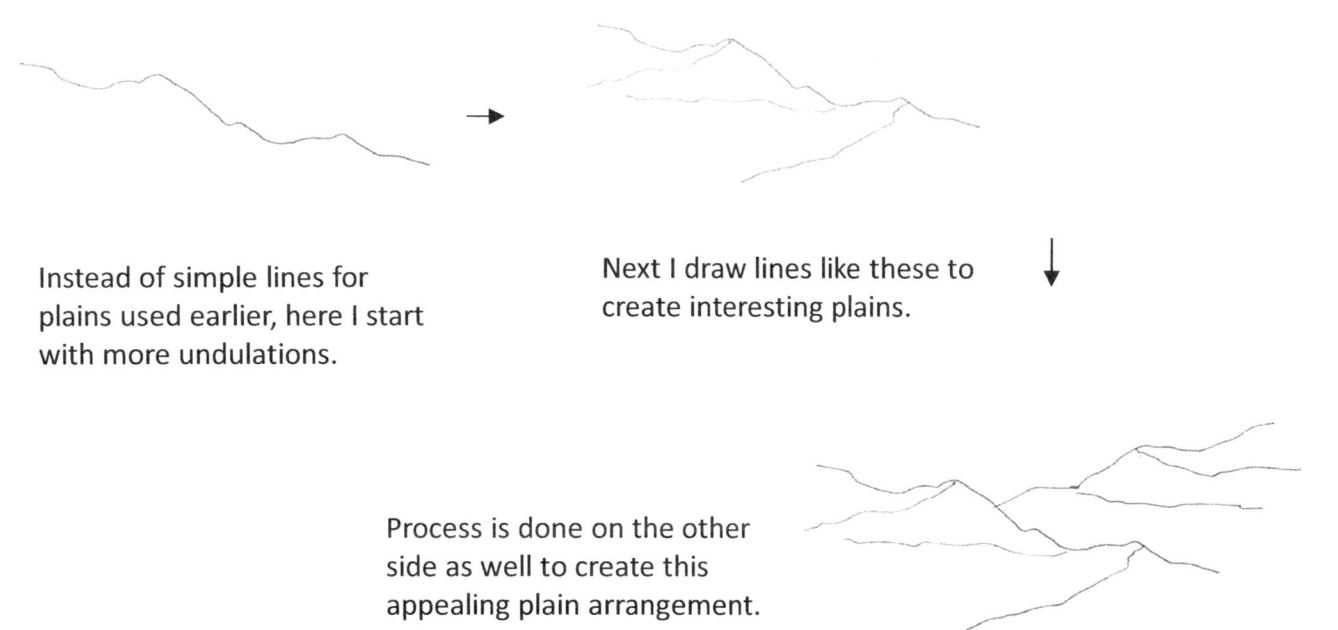

Instead of simple lines for plains used earlier, here I start with more undulations.

Next I draw lines like these to create interesting plains.

Process is done on the other side as well to create this appealing plain arrangement.

Creating More Interesting Plains, Continued:

This process can be used to create more interesting plains than based on simple lines as done earlier.

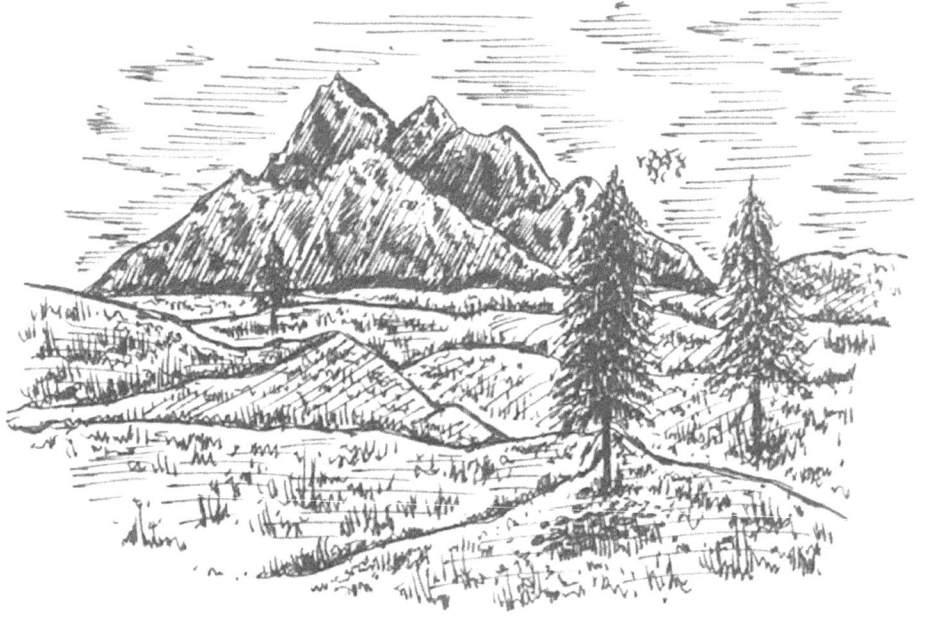

Landscape based on plain arrangement on last page.

Activity: Drawing More Interesting Plains:

Add further plains to Following starting point per instructions before.

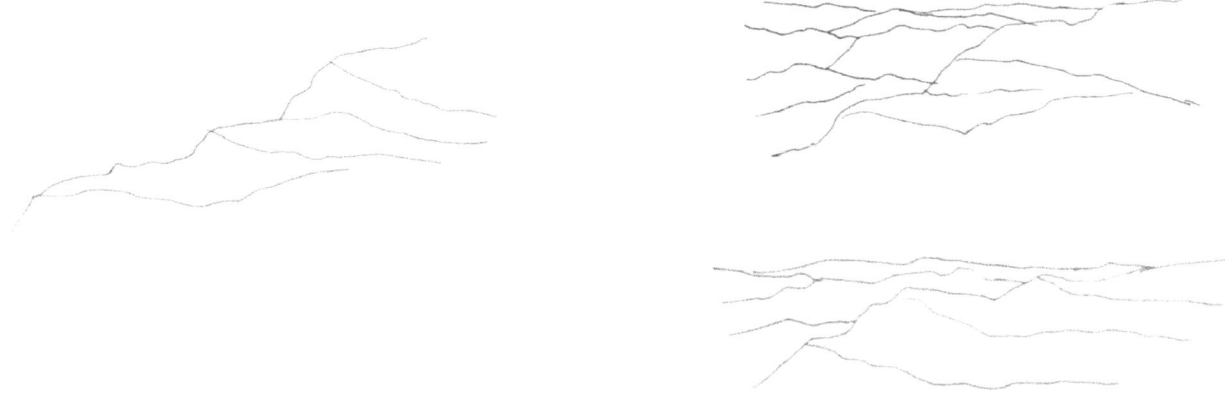

Some more examples.

Some Additional Examples:

Here are some more examples to get your creativity going.

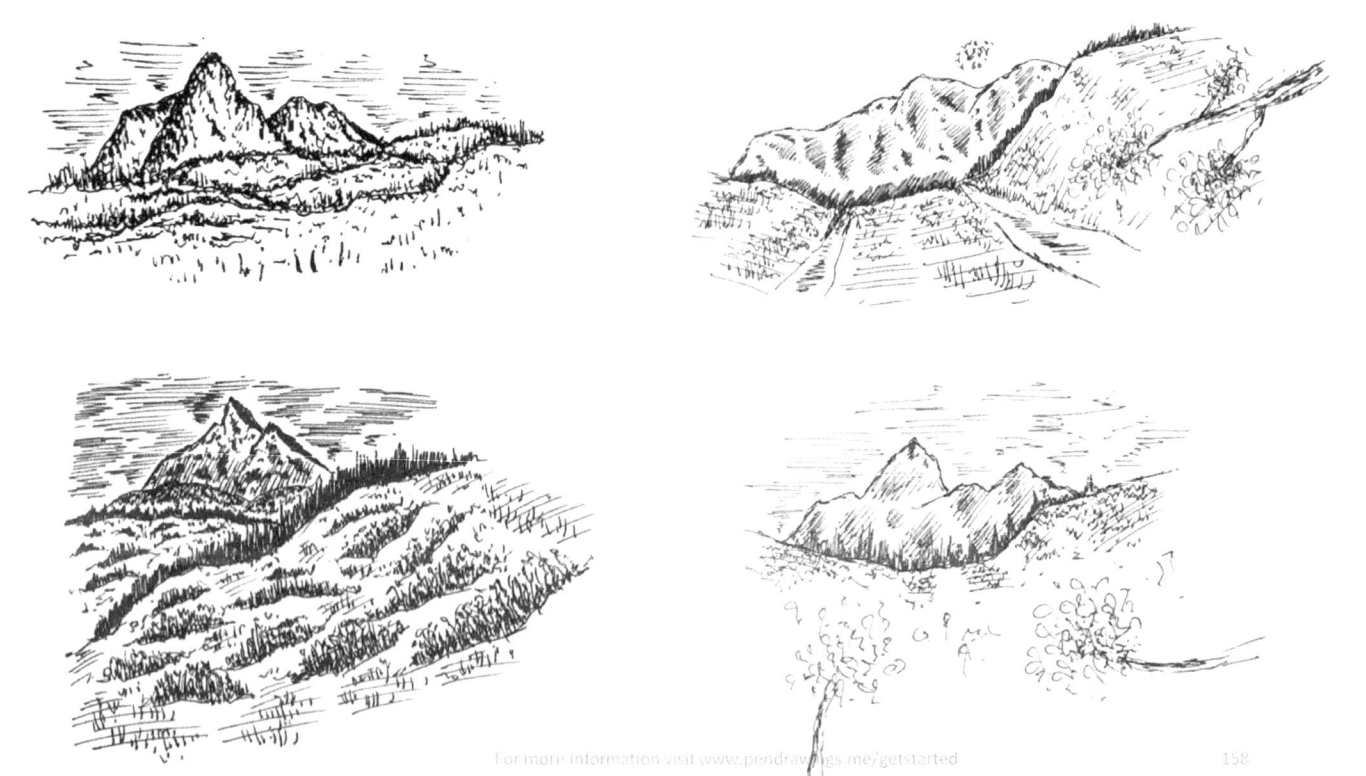

Small vs. Large Size Drawings:

As mentioned in the beginning of this workbook, the focus here is on drawing comparatively smaller sized drawings. At this smaller scale, the texture obviously in not detailed but instead the focus is on bringing out the feel with as few strokes as possible. As the size of drawing increase, more detail and texture need to be shown. Other workbooks in this series cover texturing elements of nature in detail and I invite you to consult them to further deepen your toolkit of pen and ink drawing techniques. You can find more information on other volumes at www.pendrawings.me/workbooks.

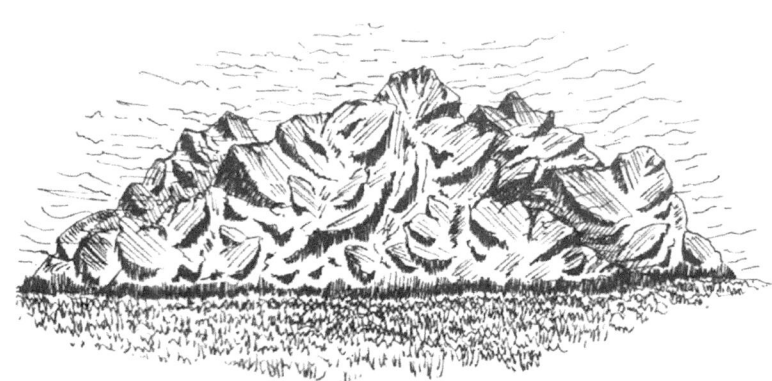

At this size, much more details on mountain can be shown.

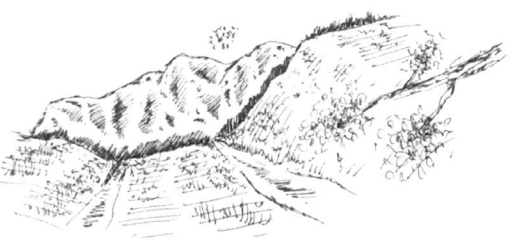

At this size, such details are not attainable.

Final Thoughts:

This is the end of this workbook but hopefully this is just the beginning of your pen and ink drawing adventure. With the approach and techniques presented in this workbook, you will be able to draw a quick and pleasing landscape any time you have a small break. Carry a pocket sketch book and a pen with you and indulge in your creativity and relaxation by attempting small sized pen and ink landscape presented in this workbook.

As with anything else, practice is key to improving. A great thing about pen drawing is that all you need is a good quality fine tip pen that can be easily carried anywhere. You don't need any fancy drawing paraphernalia or a workspace. Sit outside on a nice day on a bench in a park and with a pen and paper, try capturing the beauty of nature around you. You will learn to observe and appreciate nature more and find immense pleasure and satisfaction in capturing that beauty on a paper with simple pen strokes. Create these simple landscapes and share them with others as well. Adopt this relaxing and enjoyable hobby and it will indeed change the way you look at things around you and how you make use of time available.

In other workbooks in the series, I have covered drawing other elements of nature in detail. You can find more information about other workbooks at the following link.

www.pendrawings.me/workbooks

All feedback on improving this and other workbooks is most welcome. You can view my other works and reach me at my website, **www.pendrawings.me**

Happy Drawing,
Rahul Jain

www.ingramcontent.com/pod-product-compliance
Lightning Source LLC
Chambersburg PA
CBHW071027240526
45469CB00006BD/2123